~~MIS~~ UNDERAPPRECIATED

THE BOOK ON RE-ENGAGING THE DISENGAGED

mistakenly

Deirdre von Krauskopf

LAUNCHING YOU INC
PUBLISHING

Copyright © 2017 - Deirdre von Krauskopf

Published by Launching You inc.
All rights reserved.
This book or any portion thereof may not be reproduced or used in any manner whatsoever without the express written permission of the publisher except for the use of brief quotations in a book review or scholarly journal.

First Published in 2017 by You Inc Publishing
You Inc Publishing
Quebec, Canada
T: 1-844-333-7526

ISBN: 978-1-988995-02-1 - Paperback

Special discounts are available on quantity purchases by corporations, associations, educators, trade bookstores and wholesalers: Please contact us for more information.

Tel: (844) 333-7526; Fax: (844) 206-8446 or,

Email info@DvKPartnerGroup.com

SPECIAL THANKS TO:

Book Cover: Graphic Artist: Lynn Wyman
                 The Wyman Group
                 thewymangroupllc@gmail.com

Editor   Donna Palmer

TESTIMONIALS

"Mistakenly Underappreciated" takes seemingly complex ideas and processes and turns those ideas, quite simply, to usable forms of communication and skills one can apply to daily life. After reading this book I learned a lot about myself and methods I can apply for positive interactions between co-workers as well as customers. A very good and informative read!

~ *Christina Carter,*
  Senior Customer Service Representative, FedEx

"MISTAKENLY UNDERAPPRECIATED" is a unique book on Leadership with practical tools that can be used in any organization. It promotes a unique approach to managing the continuous and never-ending change in the workplace in manner that protects the bottom line of the company and at the same time enhances the wellbeing of the employees and staff.

The Author proposes Appreciative Inquiry as a leading tool for managing change and engaging employees, but it does not end there. The book is full of tips and tools that I think every CEO, Manager and Supervisor needs to improve workplace efficiency and maximize TEAM PRODUCTIVITY AND ENGAGEMENT. I think every leader should have a copy of this book on their shelf."

~ *Ahmad-Shah Duranai, PMP, International Bestselling Author,*
  Leadership Development and Communications Coach

Bravo Deirdre in your Guidance! Deirdre has a no-nonsense approach in leadership that is heart centered yet professional. Her personal experience and valuable contribution make this easy read a great addition to not only the corporate world but anyone who has a small business or working in the Free Enterprise world. Great Principles to live by and lead by.

~ *Lucy Niquet, Speaker, Health Coach*

This is a book that needs to be read by all those in leadership roles world-wide. Whether a multi-million-dollar corporation or a non-profit volunteer group, the approach of Appreciative Inquiry will result in positive changes within teams, service delivery, individual skill set development and the bottom-line profit.

A valuable tool that shares recommended techniques that result in win-win situations for all, laid out in a clear and direct approach by the author. It is a positive and exciting approach that will demonstrate results and turn around negative team dynamics, with strategies that can be implemented even within tight timelines. The author makes valuable use of examples to illustrate the training approach and shares her own life experiences to validate how effective this is. A must-read for all those who work with and through others. This book will greatly benefit the reader in all aspects of life, both professionally and personally.

*~ Donna Palmer, Supervisor (Ret), Design & Development,
Region of Peel*

I had the pleasure of reporting to Dee in the beginning of my career at FedEx, and to this day, I still hold that she is one of the best managers I've ever worked for. Quality driven, she accepted nothing but the best from her staff and produced results with her firm-but-fair approach to managing. She had high expectations of her employees, appreciated, and encouraged them to participate in challenging (yet manageable) work initiatives. Deirdre was always personable and maintained a pleasant demeanor even during the most stressful of days, and it was her approach that enabled her to gain the trust and confidence of her staff.

Motivational, empathetic, and humble, she was definitely a "people's manager" unafraid to go to bat for her employees - and yet she somehow managed to find a balance between pleasing her people and pleasing the business, a feat only accomplished when a manager is effective in engaging her staff to work towards the same goal. Deirdre knows the key to running an efficient, happy, successful team!

~ Abi Sampson ~ FedEx Customer Service Representative

*"Treat people as if they were what they ought to be,
and you help them become
what they are capable of being."
~Johann Wolfgang von Goethe*

FOREWARD

Written By: Lisa Duarte
Director, Marketing and Communications
Region of Peel

I had the pleasure of mentoring Deirdre as she reported to me as a Strategic Manager and Project Manager as well as watching her success in her roles under different Directors and Commissioners. Whether managing teams directly or indirectly there is a talent to motivating and coaching the best out people. The tools and tactics provided in Mistakenly Underappreciated were proven effective time and again by her leadership style and through her mentoring and coaching of the managers, supervisors, and teams that reported to her. This book is not industry-specific; it will aid any team success. Ask anyone who worked for, or with Deirdre and they will confirm, she gets things done and her people are loyal and enthusiastic fans.

When you meet Deirdre, you will quickly realize there is nothing overtly touchy-feely about her; she resonates a powerful, "all business" presence. However, as learned while she worked for me and others you will soon come to understand she has a deep respect and desire to bring the best out of people, even those she influences indirectly. Her knowledge is born from a deep understanding of human and organizational behavior from which her education shines through.

Deirdre's career experience is a unique and varied mix of leadership roles, developed from openness to take on any opportunity offered with dedication and drive to gain expertise that is formable to see in action. In her words though, it is the ability to lead driven and coachable teams that led to her repeated success. You must care about your team's progress and growth as well as attain the organizational objectives.

In this book, she shares some of her tactics that will help anyone achieve better success, not just leaders.

In reading Mistakenly Underappreciated, I have a clearer understanding of how she accomplished this. While "employee engagement" is a key focus of many industries strategic plans and human resource key objectives few managers truly comprehend the financial impact of disengagement and turnover costs. The slow drip of "quit and stay" attitudes on productivity and collaboration along with absenteeism and time abuse has a significant impact on budget success. The statistics that prove this are throughout this book and give you and your teams powerful insights in an area not often given much focus.

Leading a positive culture in today's workplace environment is more challenging; the days of 30-year careers has been lessening and will continue to do so. Motivation to achieve organizational success and avoid costly turn over means the leadership model must incorporate engagement into their overall and department level culture. This information is missing from most educational degrees, and the long path of learning by trial and error has a high price tag to leader success and the company's bottom line.

The elements of communication and emotional intelligence are an even lesser strength in many new, and frankly, tenured employees within the workforce. It is incumbent on the leadership to bridge the learning in these critical and "not so soft" skills. While we all grow our strength in these crucial areas of success over time, having a supervisor, manager and the organizational leadership place a priority on them will significantly aid productivity and bottom-line results faster. I liked how these concepts were clearly described, and examples, ideas, and tactics provided to educate the reader on how to get there expediently.

The chapter on change fatigue particularly fits in the ever-evolving corporate cultures in most industries as we struggle to keep up with the technological advances that not only impact efficiency and financial results but are a vital demand to the customers we serve.

Being a certified change management professional aided Deirdre's success, but her method was more about ensuring the operational leaders were equally competent and engaged in the process and that showed in her results.

Having leadership that engages and motivates their teams to embrace and gain enthusiasm for what she called the "next" practice, not just the best practice is worth the cost of the training program mentioned in her book. All her training sessions were well received across departments with enthusiasm and glowing feedback. Creating a positive momentum in change is a talent every leader needs to attain.

It was interesting to read the sections related to hiring and on-boarding as Deirdre was a sought-after co-interviewer for many department heads and human resource staff. Her ability to make the candidate comfortable and then gently probe and explore responses to gain the best understanding of an individual resulted in great hires that at times would be otherwise be overlooked. Her questioning technique, shared in chapter 7, separated the candidates with excellent resumes but little substance from the candidates that would come in coachable, willing, and able to get the job done.

I highly recommend this book for any level of leadership and her training program even more. Aiding all this information with the neuroscience of human behavior and motivation creates an eye-opening impact for teams and leaders alike.

"People ~ Service ~ Profit"
If you invest in your people,
they will provide a superior service
which will generate profit,
which in turn allows you to invest in your people.
~Frederick W. Smith, CEO/Founder, FedEx

INTRODUCTION

Leadership isn't about perfection or authoritative control over someone. If no one wants to follow you, then you are not a leader. Leadership is a privilege, its empowering, and most importantly, it is a rewarding honor to watch those you coach, mentor, and guide as they grow and develop into the best version of themselves. A person who honestly feels appreciated will always do more than what is expected of them.

This book started as a free eBook giveaway when I facilitated or coached corporate clients through Change Initiatives and Strategic Planning exercises. Often the questions and issues that arose were repetitive and attendees would ask for different tools. With limited time at the moment, I started writing out helpful insights and voila, in time, a book was born. One of the things I noticed was how hard some leaders were on themselves when it came to managing change and dealing with challenging employee-manager situations.

You may recognize that the book title mimics the Bushism word *"misunderestimate"* that has found its way into the Urban Dictionary, as has "misunderappreciated" since I began writing this book. I am aware that the grammar elite among us may be cringing, my apologies. The play on words lightheartedly emphasizes that most leaders are not under-appreciating their teams on purpose. They simply "don't know what they don't know."

Many leaders are mistakenly using old, ineffective managing techniques in an era where constant change is the new norm and the 30-year stable career, considered something from a dinosaur age by our up-and-coming workforce. "*Misunderappreciating*," or mistakenly under-appreciating our valuable and fickle talent pool is a genuine issue in organizations today.

This book focuses on how to use a fantastic tool to re-engage teams, so they are ready for the evolution of your organization. It starts with appreciating them and follows with the demise of "change fatigue." Why is it so important to learn these skills? Gallup Polls and leading surveys show:

- **51% of employees are looking to leave their current jobs.**

- **76% of employees would work more if they had an empathic employer.**

- **70% of employees say that motivation and morale would improve "massively" with managers saying thank you more.**

- **63% of disengaged employees don't trust their manager.**

- **42% of employees feel their leaders do not contribute to a positive company culture.**

- **40% of "Quit and Stay" or "Employee Prisoners" report their manager provides little encouragement to do their best, and,**

- **Only 24% of workers are HIGHLY ENGAGED… GLOBALLY!**

On the positive side, it is well documented those businesses tracking employee experience indicate an average of **10% increase in customer ratings.** Investing in training to improve teams means you are investing in positive customer experiences as well. Your employees can help or hinder your brand! Statistics also show engaged employees help drive sales. When someone feels they are a valued part of a broader system, their quality of effort improves. **Companies tracking this saw a 20% increase in sales.**

This book will provide you with excellent learnings to use in business environments where change is the new norm and not an occasional event. The tools will help re-engage teams that are not serving a collective goal. It will equally serve among multigenerational workgroups who, by employee engagement surveys, tell us the same thing; they want to be recognized and appreciated for what they do.

Though it is not a new concept, many times during training or coaching clients on Change Management or Strategic Initiatives I have learned the contents of this book are not well known to many leaders. Therefore, employees are "mistakenly underappreciated."

So many people fail to ascend to their highest potential and even become the prophesied "bad employee" as a result of a leader who focused too much on their negatives. It is important to acknowledge that few leaders learn the skill of how to coach the best out of others. A missed opportunity that has significant costs to an organization, I hope this book is the beginning of changing that for your company.

Most of you want to be the kind of leader that staff enjoy working with and admire. As an influencer, you want people to respect you. Some readers will be seeking ways to make good teams exceptional, some of you are inheriting a workgroup with a challenging history, others will be searching for an answer to an underperforming or toxic team.

When people aren't following you with enthusiasm, then something is damaged, missing or lacking. When you start learning what "you" can do to improve this, then you are focusing on the only thing you can change, you! Whatever reason you are here the tools within will help transform your group, which is the ultimate goal. After all, without your team, you have no one and nothing to lead.

We now know we are rarely taught the soft skills needed for success through our standard education or employment journey. Now it is time to understand it is these very skills that define exceptional leadership and teamwork.

Some arrive at leadership from a place where they earned it from being an outstanding staff member or from tenured experience. Their methods of productivity worked well for them, and they expect others to be like them without understanding how to motivate and coach those who are not. Time and again we have seen that being a fantastic staff member does not automatically translate to being a good supervisor, manager, or leader.

The best leaders have an awareness that not everyone thinks likeminded, and that is a good thing. When you cultivate and honor a variety of viewpoints, personality, and work styles your staff will evolve into a more cohesive and engaged team.

My team mantra has always been "if I am the smartest person in the room there's a problem, as collectively we are much smarter." Outside of action-adventure movies, there is no "one-man Army." This belief cultivates a team where people feel appreciated and valued for their unique contribution.

Appreciative Inquiry is a must-have tool for every leader. I have found it particularly useful for re-engaging teams that are disengaged or toxic, but please note, it's not an overnight fix, it takes time to build authentic relationships, but it works.

DvK Partner Group's training build high-performance teams that are motivated to achieve corporate objectives. The focus of this book is Appreciative Inquiry; a critical tool that assists new and tenured leaders to develop their team's skills in communication, innovation, agility, adaptability, and critical thinking.

The people in our influence circle deserve to be "heard, understood, respected and accepted," (~ James MacNeil), and you, as a leader, deserve the same in return.

Table of Contents

TESTIMONIALS — 3

FOREWARD — 7

INTRODUCTION — 10

ACKNOWLEDGMENTS — 19

HOW DOES ANYTHING GET DONE AROUND HERE? — 21

WHAT'S GROOMED, BLOOMS! — 33

LEADING A POSITIVE CULTURE — 49

TO THINK IS TO BE — 59

THE POWER OF WORDS — 73

NO MORE CHANGE FATIGUE! — 89

ON-BOARDING SPECIAL SAUCE — 103

REALITY CHECK — 127

THE VISIONARY LEADER — 143

INFLUENCING WITH EMOTIONAL INTELLIGENCE — 159

~ ANNE M. MULCAHY — 172

THE "ME" FACTOR   **173**

INQUISITIVENESS ~ THE SECRET TO POSITIVE CHANGE
    189

DEVELOPING COACHABLE TEAMS   **207**

IT STARTS WITH YOU!   **221**

ABOUT THE AUTHOR   **236**

Leadership is not about a title or a designation.
It's about impact, influence, and inspiration.
Impact involves getting results.
Influence is about spreading the passion you have for your work,
and you have to inspire teammates and customers.
~ Robin Sharma

ACKNOWLEDGMENTS

Christina Carter, awesome Senior Editor with a refreshing "tell it straight" manner.

Donna Palmer, Editor and amazing at catching phrasing "fails." Your ease of reading is thanks to this lovely lady!

Those closest to me who had to endure "It is ready to go to print, oh wait, I want to rewrite this part again" and again, and again!

To one of my business partners, D. James Lauber, an expert in "wordplay," for the clever title.

To James MacNeil, who created the Verbal Aikido Program and licensed out its use while he pursued new endeavors.

As a Global Partner I have spent countless hours helping our small team of 22 Licensed Partners build their businesses to great successes across North America and beyond, I am grateful for this group of awesome people.

I am blessed to be sharing my accumulated knowledge with corporations, my Going Beyond the Call ~ Trauma-Informed work with public safety professionals, and many other customized courses. This has been the best possible post retirement career I could hope for. Thank you to all participants and clients!

CHAPTER 1

HOW DOES ANYTHING GET DONE AROUND HERE?

A pessimist sees the difficulty in everything...
An optimist sees the opportunity in everything.
~Winston Churchill

Have you ever wondered *"how does anything get done around here?"* Imagine your workplace as a mini city unto itself. Think of departments as little districts, each with individual political hierarchies and cultural norms. Within, lives a mix of suburbs thinking their area has the highest value or is the most important. At its worst, you have a collection of rival regions acting like competing High Schools. They all may be part of a collective "City" but each entirely internalized in their own little world or what we commonly refer to as "silos."

Organizations are designed with the idealism they are a living entity, composed of individuals working hard toward a common goal. However, far too often that is not the case, and the smallest hints of dysfunction and uncooperativeness left untended can grow into a dramatic or unproductive mess.

I was labelled a "fixer" by several organizations. I would take over a "problem workgroup" and within 3-6 months consistently evolve the team into a productive, happier group, measured through the change from low to high scores on employee surveys.

Often, I would be forewarned about one or more "problem employee" that needed to be dealt with firmly. Funny enough, time and again, the "problem" wasn't the employee but the process in which they had been managed.

I saw multiple efforts to band-aid the issue or "process improve" the situation with efficiency-based solutions that segregated and micromanaged each employee, often to the point of losing the critical problem in the mix. If your team is fractured and underappreciated, then process improvement efforts will likely fail.

When a workgroup feels micromanaged, a lack of encouragement, their ideas are dismissed, or overall, that their contribution is unvalued, you will likely begin to hear specific terms. Terms like change fatigue, disgruntled or lack of employee engagement or at its worst, a poisoned or toxic work environment.

The result is too much time spent focused on trying to performance manage "process steps" over the real issues of individual human behavior and team dynamics. Workgroups become fractured while unified contribution and attaining higher objectives get lost in the weeds. That does not bode well for a leader's sustainable success.

When key performance indicators or workgroup efficiency objectives are unrealized, the first thought is usually not "How is the environmental wellness impacting our team?" I have left the question rather broad as it may or may not include leadership as the source of the problem. It could be the result of unclear expectations from a higher level.

It could also be a workplace bully, or other peer factors that have disenfranchised the workgroup. It may be an ongoing frustration with other areas with whom they interact. It could encompass corporate change initiatives or recent negative public or political influence, etc....

Seeking the answer to this question should be a priority to ensure you understand and accept the critical value of a healthy work environment to aid productive results. It does not mean you overlook standard management assessments like reviewing job functions, setting clear expectations, and having consistent evaluation standards. Nor do you ignore the organizational and departmental objectives or any other explicit barriers to success.

This tactic will prove much more successful than jumping to an "employee performance improvement process" without a broader situational scan. Appraisal of work effort is only one aspect of an effective Performance Management system. If you just focus on that one aspect, you will often fall short of a high performing team.

If you wish a tool to help with that, the S.W.O.T. Analysis (Strengths, Weaknesses, Opportunities, Threats) and the P.E.S.T.L.E. (Political, Economic, Social, Technological, Legal and Environmental) exercise may be of assistance and templates are readily available online. Under the environmental section ensure you consider leadership, change initiatives, peer-to-peer, cross-department, and any external agency influence.

With a SWOT analysis, you will be reviewing all aspects of performance management. These will lead to an ongoing communication strategy between team and leadership that establishes clear expectations and the measurable requirements of a job well done.

When a team is unsuccessful for an extended period, it is common to arrive at a leadership change eventually. If the situation is dire, the executive team may hire a leader known for being a change agent. A pinch hitter of sorts, to turn things around. Often tasked to lead a workgroup in this situation it was my experience that the outgoing manager had made efforts to achieve the efficiency results required.

Commonly, their heavy reliance on performance appraisal-based methodology did not resonate well with their team. In most cases, high frustration with the workgroup was commonplace with fingers pointing in every direction but towards themselves as a leader. The same scenario replayed time and again.

This underlying truth is why I put a strong focus on these "soft skills" when I retired from the corporate world and began facilitating and speaking on transformational change for measurable results. The strategic communication and emotional intelligence skills we teach in our workshops are rarely part of higher education curriculum or leadership programs. While some leaders and team members have these skills naturally, far more, do not.

The Appreciative Inquiry process is a practical and fast method to use as you assess the contributions of the team members and build ongoing relationships with them. From this place of rapport, you can begin to design clear expectations and create an understanding of what everyone is working towards which produces the change needed for measurable productivity gains. Helping form the foundation for a superior and fulsome performance management process that creates winning teams.

You may consider your own experiences as you have moved throughout your career. Which leaders do you remember most when thinking back? The leaders who respected and appreciated your efforts? The ones that created an environment for you to develop your skills. Or were your first thoughts drawn to those leaders who did not support you, or who micromanaged and ignored contributions you felt deserved recognition?

Individuals look to the designated leader for inspiration, guidance, direction, and they want the leader to look at them for the contributions they provide. Individuals are quite often emotionally hungry for acknowledgment of what they do well before they are open to learning and growing their skills. If folks feel incompetent or believe they are undervalued, they may find it a challenge to be coachable and open to new ways of doing things. They may lack the desire to participate in actions that move the group towards the goals, and they may build resistance to listening to constant corrective measures.

This under-appreciation creates disgruntled and often disruptive employees. Have you come across workgroups that are a collective of predominately unhappy, unwell, unmotivated, squabbling individuals? Have you noticed the energy and significant time that these adverse situations take from working towards the organization's objectives? How about the typical escalation meetings between management and labor relations or Human Resources?

What you are witnessing is a lack of soft skills, which is understandable as most organizations do not put a focus on them until it threatens the bottom line. Which, statistics show, is actually an immediate and ongoing issue but not always recognized until it is quite significant. Countless articles and studies show these skills are critical to sustainable success in leadership and employability, yet they are rarely considered mandatory training elements.

The foundational aspect of any role, in any industry, is Emotional Intelligence and Communications Strategies. Very few positions are isolated from interacting with other people. Skills learned from these core aspects aid both work and personal interactions, which also positively impacts wellness. It also aids maturity and understanding on how to manage stress, gain resilience, build adaptability to change and begin the journey to higher mindfulness overall. Appreciative Inquiry falls under communications strategies for leading productive and engaged teams.

Most often, soft skills are all those qualities we tend to learn through experience. Some individuals acquire these skills with a more natural or innate talent, while many never quite grasp the importance unless directly taught the science behind it and the tools to implement. While a few of these skills may be part of a higher curriculum education in some fields, the majority of programs do not teach any of them. These skills influence our behaviors, attitudes and personalities and aid both our critical thinking and innovative, creative sides.

The emphasis in education is on the technical and hard skills, yet attitude, awareness, and the ability to be part of a cohesive team are some of the performance issues your management complains about the most. In leadership, it is even more critical as you are not only responsible for your performance but the success of those reporting to you.

Having a high IQ or outstanding street smarts will only get you so far without the soft skills that enable your brilliance to be heard, understood, and respected. Often the more technical or analytical your hard skillset is, the weaker your soft skills are. I have worked with absolutely brilliant Engineers, IT Professionals, Lawyers, Accountants and Project Managers who failed in their ability to build and motivate their teams or communicate effectively because of this.

I have further watched them transform overnight with our core soft skills training program or one-on-one coaching. Once they understand that there is a science behind it with tangible benefits towards their objectives and outcomes the more, they want to learn.

Don't get me wrong; I love a robust, measurable

process! KPI's, Strategic Plans, Business Model Canvas Planning, Gantt charts, Work Plans, these all make me tingle with joy as I am a productivity driven human being and have enjoyed a successful career out of cultivating this expertise.

However, what provided me consistent and continual success in developing the "what, where, why, and how" of those roles wasn't the ease of facts, figures, processes, charts, and budgets; those are easy to manage and quite clear to understand. It is the magic of "who" that creates success, that "people factor" far too often left to a lower tier priority. If a leader cannot learn to motivate and empower others, they will struggle to build and maintain a team that achieves cohesive collaboration and meets strategic objectives.

This book and the offered training program are part of a developing series. Great leadership develops when following a path of continual learning, coaching and mentorship. Appreciative Inquiry, in this age of constant change, is a critical tool to learn and apply. It helps teams thrive in a continually evolving workplace; whether to maintain competitiveness, understand new technology, modernizing processes, adapting to new and altering marketplaces, right-sizing, or restructuring.

You build the awareness of change in an empowered, contributive way while continuing a cornerstone philosophy of recognizing and appreciating your team's contributions along the way. From this point, you can guide the conversation through a change management process.

Remaining open to learn and consider new adaptation ideas, provide some ownership with the implementation, and build interest in the change for those impacted. Regardless of any initial grumbling, employees are more likely to want to be involved in a change process than just told to accept a new reality.

As an example, I was contracted to work with a team of managers on a departmental merging that had gone terribly wrong. I encountered substantial absenteeism among employees, staff regularly getting up and walking out of integration meetings and the initiative timelines were far behind schedule. Certified in the ADKAR model of change management we began reviewing their project plan with a new approach to their change strategy.

While presenting the critical aspects of this model which are, Awareness, Desire, Knowledge, Action, and Reinforcement one manager said: "we sent an email, so they ARE aware!"

Not the most useful or respectful approach when significant changes to the way of doing business were about to unfold. We stopped with the ADKAR process, had a quick meeting with the executive who hired me. They quickly agreed to a switch in training, and we re-started with our core soft skills program and some Appreciative Inquiry coaching first.

After the training, the team of managers transformed. They understood that with a narrow focus on the process they did not realize or consider the human impact underlying the change. They had inadvertently caused the delays and adverse reactions believing it wasn't a big deal. The plan did not consider the culture and customs of the merging workgroups, nor the emotional impacts significant change had on people. The process also didn't explicitly outline the roles and responsibilities, so people were unsure where they fit in.

They rallied to get the training for the transitioning teams to "reset" their ineffective approach and move forward on the right track. We found that blending the ADKAR change process and the foundational soft skills training with managers and staff together was the answer. Immediate improvements in the transition process planning were noted. Cooperation and sharing skyrocketed, and the teams came together with an eagerness to be involved. The leaders were now using Appreciative Inquiry to value the individuals; the ideas started flowing to build highly effective transition plans.

Sometimes in our urgency to meet continually changing markets and technological requirements we forget that proper process management requires two critical aspects to be successful. One side is all the leaders and team who are part of the planning and executing of change, the technical process and management of the event. The other side is all those impacted who can significantly help, or they can substantially hinder the change process. Most importantly, these are the people who are carrying out the result of the change and delivering to end users, and that directly impacts your customer experience and bottom line.

Change is often an emotional and stressful event, even though it is easily argued as the only constant in the world. Any process that has an emotional impact is best managed with excellent soft skills and leading your teams through it can be considerably assisted with an Appreciative Inquiry focus.

*The test of a leader lies
in the reaction and response of his followers.
He should not have to impose authority.
Bossiness in itself never made a leader.
He must make his influence felt by example
and the instilling of confidence in his followers.
The greatness of a leader is measured by
the achievements of the led.
This is the ultimate test of his effectiveness.*

~General Omar Bradley

CHAPTER 2

WHAT'S GROOMED, BLOOMS!

Look for the best in people all the time.
If you look for the best,
you're going to draw out the best.

~*Richard Branson, Virgin Group*

How does Appreciative Inquiry have the ability to change an entire organization by changing its people? Through positive questioning to start. Employees will be more encouraged to move in a positive direction when they are part of the discovery process. Begin discussions by recognizing the strengths and values of what the employee does well. Then lead them through questions to allow the employee to identify what could use some improvement.

With the positive aspects identified, you can move to "so tell me, what are the top three challenges you are finding with ABC Project?" With comfort established, they will start to bring up the issues. In a safe environment, they are more likely to identify where they could do better or how they had a challenge with another area.

As they identify a concern area, note it and continue with probing questions "what do you think are some options to improve that?"

You will be pleasantly surprised that they will most often have great ideas to self-correct on their own and now have considerable buy-in as it's entirely their idea.

If they are stuck on a solution after you have asked them to solve it on their own, they are more likely to be open to mentoring and the answers you offer. Even if they need corrective behavior or performance direction, they remain more open because they were given an opportunity to solve the problem and could not do so.

The mindset is now one of fixing something together or asking for help, not just going into the boss's office and "getting crapped on." This simple method of identifying an improvement area will transform individuals, thereby transforming organizations.

Too often the discussion approach used by a leader initially jumps on what is wrong. Does this sound familiar: "Do you know why I called you in here today?" The employee's ego state usually flares reactively to either fear, confusion, or pride. In an instant, the amygdala can activate into a "fight, flight or freeze" response. Alternatively, they may withdraw, start creating excuses and blame others to deflect or jump into a full-on combative mode before the next words are uttered. Their emotions are triggered without any actual context as to the situation at hand.

I teach Law Enforcement agencies a training program of emotional intelligence, advanced communications, body language, and the philosophy of the non-confrontational martial art Aikido. It is a version of our foundational soft skills training, but the focus is on "pre-escalation" in non-violent interactions, building a collaborative community and interpersonal relationships.

I share this as an example as it is understood and recognized by most people and drives the point home. Think of a time when you have observed live, or on TV, as a Police Officer roars up to a scene. The sirens are blaring; they jump out of the car, lights still going and approach a bystander, brusquely demanding information.

Although this is a dramatized account, I want you to feel a "bigger than life" show of authority. We can understand if they are arriving at a bank robbery or a major crisis incident. It would be entirely expected in this scenario, we would want our Law Enforcement to be commanding and in charge, to make things safe again. That explicit authority is a crucial part of the training, to take command and control of every scene they manage. Authority and power do not necessarily require an aggressive stance though, once trained in pre-escalation interaction management; they have more tools and options to adapt their approach to the situation.

What if their goal is expecting a measure of cooperation in order to assess a scene quickly and determine their next actions? Then that overtly powerful show of authority could have an opposite effect. We get into the neuroscience more deeply in workshops, but here, in the highest summary, I will share the basics. The amygdala, in response to intensive new stimuli, especially a threat, will set off a series of notifications to other body response systems and a stress reaction is likely to occur.

In stress-provoking situations, fear, pride, or confusion become the predominant emotion likely aroused, and the interaction can become far more adversarial and uncooperative than it needs to be. When someone is fearful, anxious, threatened or confused the following Ego State Communication is not likely going to remain in a rational, calm, and logical state. An officer may have increased the odds that escalation or lack of cooperation will occur where it might have been avoided.

Police still need to be "at the ready" for anything that comes at them. For survival and protection of others, they must be quick and skillfully prepared to adjust tactics on an escalating scale of response. In this, they are trained very well, contrary to the training they receive for engaging people cooperatively to maintain logical, adult Ego State conversations. Yet, this is how they will best gain insights from reluctant or hesitant citizens and attain their interactive and investigative objectives.

Pre-escalation skills are learning the communication strategies required when the objective is to achieve rapport and understanding. To listen and respond with a goal of gaining beneficial information and striving to initiate the building blocks of trust for cooperative interactions. Now back to the workplace, can you envision how useful this skill may be for managing challenging employees, customers, or toxic workgroups?

Let's add an overview of the underlying brain science of

why equal stimuli can be interpreted so differently between us. The Amygdala is a small almond shape right next to the hippocampus (memory center) are part of the limbic system. It is the part of our brain that leads our emotional responses, fear, pride, confusion, anxiety, anger and also pleasure, excitement to new stimuli. The limbic system is the gatekeeper for all incoming stimulation.

Yes, as popular Google searches will show, it assesses threats. However more modern neuroscience research confirms it also scans for anything new, exciting, highly positive, or even things that are unusual or unknown.

All inputs that could hurt, hinder, or help you in life calculated in mere milliseconds triggers the psychological and physiological response systems. All before much-considered thought happens from our Neocortex, where our reasoning and logic resides. When that reactionary sequence senses a threat your fight, flight or freeze response set off a chain reaction before the hippocampus can add what we already may know to balance our response and before the cortex can put some logical reasoning to our response.

Therefore, unless we learn about this response system and train our brain to manage it, our "knee-jerk" emotional reaction will show before any logic comes into play. Once all three levels of our brain are engaged in a series of checks and balances to assess the continued need for "fight, flight or freeze" or de-escalation you have better control of your response.

What does that mean? Some may watch a Police Officer approach in a domineering way and attach no emotional value to it. Their perception and experience interpret it as expected. Another, through direct or indirect experience or social conditioning, may have a fear-based response. In our workplace, one employee may view change as exciting and embrace it with eager curiosity while another will have a dramatic fear-based reaction.

The Amygdala attaches emotional stimuli to our memories which attaches a level of importance to the impacting moments in our life, whether positive or negative. This explains how one person may have a near irrational fear of a snake or spider while another does not. It is also why traumatic situations that happen from infancy onward stay with us for a lifetime if left unaddressed.

Fear, of course, has a higher "sticking" factor as it is viewed as a threat. Our most basic human response is to avoid things that we consider dangerous. As an example, if a member of someone's family lived in poverty, suffered from multiple layoffs, or had a series of poor working experiences, then they may grow up with a heightened fear of changes in the workplace. Even if they have no personal or rational reasoning for their fear reaction, it is still there, and it is very real to them.

The problem comes when our reaction happens at the Amygdala stage before the rest of the brain system assesses the larger picture. We may have already reacted in an emotionalized way that has led to a counter-reaction by the other person, and with the chemicals still coursing through our veins, it becomes much easier to become re-triggered.

This is why when we are in a lousy mood, things that do not usually irritate us, do. It is also why if someone snaps at us; we can quickly snap back without thinking, the trigger, re-trigger cycle beings and an argument quickly ensues.

If we train ourselves to stop our instant reaction response for a millisecond or two, we are then influenced by the Hippocampus, the "memory center" section of the brain. This area scans our life and social knowledge and provides input from all your past experiences and inputs. Yes, all of them, from childhood to present. All the knowledge, emotional moments and perceptions gathered from experiences with parents, teachers, guardians, siblings, bullies, previous bosses, good and bad relationships, media, culture, etc. Within milliseconds all these inputs build on a person's perception of the current moment in time.

Then, the neocortex will logically assess and provide you with the best possible option based on all those inputs; the cortex is what makes us human and able to control our brain. The rational, logical mind cannot compete with a highly emotionalized mind though. Visualize a teeter-totter; you have emotional or logical. One or the other, one is at the top the other is on the bottom.

The Cortex, our rational, controlled self, is the last to enter the sequence, and far too often, after the initial emotional response or knee-jerk reaction that expresses fear, pride or confusion has already been released. It is now harder, without awareness and training, to stop the emotional spiral and allow the logic to enter and take command.

As a leader this insight means an authoritative approach may invoke an escalated emotional situation that wouldn't have happened with a more objective-based approach. Most people, without training, practice or significant experience will find their rational mind is not the first responder under heightened stress.

To hinder logic further, in those initial seconds old memories of similar stressful moments are reviewed along with memories acquired through others; including social media, movies etc., and all the emotions of those situations are subconsciously thrown into the current response action.

When someone in authority is raising the internal emotional alarm, there may also be an unconscious bias about that person in power or their perceived position. The distressed person has no direct emotional management conditioning for it, and often they aren't even consciously aware that it is part of their reaction.

Why? Because when one perceives that another has a power over them and could do them some harm (arrested, hurt, reprimand, fire), whether they have any direct personal history of issues in the past, they will likely not handle the interaction very well.

Some people have more rational based responses naturally or over time. One would have this ability through Emotional Intelligence that has developed from their nature and nurture influences, critical thinking skills, specialized training, or age. As we grow older those memories, we pull from are more balanced.

We go into the brain science in greater depth during our workshops, but hopefully, this gives you some insight on "why" people overreact and get so worked up about things at work. More importantly, why it is critical to weave Emotional Intelligence training into your team development, so they are more capable of adapting to change and difficult conversations.

As you see, I started weaving in the correlation between police and team leaders. There is a correlation, on an immediate emotional reaction level, aside from the extent of unconscious bias, as both are in a position of authority over another person.

Therefore, an authoritative approach which invokes a negative emotion that triggers fear, pride or confusion will likely result in a challenging, uncooperative, potentially emotionalized conversation. If your objective is to gain a cooperative or positive outcome, you will need to manage your approach.

Police learn to keep their emotions in check, mostly due to an above average and consistent experience with emotionally distraught people. Most Leaders do not have a daily dose of high emotion to deal with or learn from so there is the added consideration of counter ego triggering when responding to an emotionalized employee.

Think of a time when someone's reaction invokes a thought of "*How dare they talk back to me like that!*" "*Why are they overreacting?*" Or "*Are they going to lose it on me?*"

You can imagine this quickly moves the conversation away from objective and logic based as both parties are triggered into emotionalized, ego-driven states.

When I hear a leader say someone is a *"difficult person"* I often wonder if we asked that person, would they say the leader was difficult too? Likely they are triggering each other.

Leadership, in my opinion, needs to have many tactical approaches. If your goal is to create a capable, engaged, productive team or you want an objective, performance-based conversation then the authority driven approach is not going to get you very far. This is especially true with the younger generations, where most were not raised to respect authority just because someone holds a particular position.

Keep in mind Appreciative Inquiry is a communications strategy, one of many in your toolbox. It will not always be the most appropriate tool, such as at a suspension or termination meeting after all queries and intervention work has been completed. If your goal is to change behavior or improve employee performance, then this technique shifts away from only looking at their problems and deficiencies to a more empowered perspective. It is much more advantageous to focus on strengths and successes and then add in guided questions to introduce the performance concerns. This allows the employee to self-visualize and self-identify the problematic aspects.

When someone can visualize their own shortcomings, with their own words, they are much more apt to offer solutions that resonate internally and then commit more readily to the agreed upon changes. This useful communication tool will strengthen team relationships throughout an organization.

Wharton business school management professor Gregory Shea says, *"leaders can quickly turn workgroups toxic through the misguided belief that being harsh and unforgiving is a productive way to manage every employee."*[i]

Leaders don't need to bully to impact productivity. Christine Porath, a Georgetown University professor of management, and Christine Pearson, a professor at the Thunderbird School of Global Management at Arizona State University, conducted a study on incivility.[ii] It found incivility demoralizes people and they retaliate. Of those responding they had been treated poorly:

- **38% decreased their quality of work.**

- **47% deliberately decreased time spent working.**

- **78% said their commitment to the organization declined; and,**

- **25% admitted to taking their frustrations out on customers.**

Conversely, imagine an environment where leadership focuses on seeing and promoting the best in people. A thriving workplace where you are given the opportunity to take ownership of your personal and team areas of improvement.

An environment where your positive changes and efforts are acknowledged. This communication strategy tool in your toolbox will assist with building this level of employee engagement.

A Gallup Poll[iii] identified employees want a lot more from their managers with statistics identifying:

> *"Employees whose managers are open and approachable are more engaged ... A productive workplace is one in which employees feel safe to experiment, challenge, share and support one another. The best managers get to know their employees and help them feel comfortable talking about any subject and able to approach the manager with any question."*
>
> *"Employees whose managers focus on their strengths are more engaged. In "strengths-based" cultures, employees learn their roles more quickly, produce more and significantly better work, stay with their*

company longer and are more engaged."

"Conversely the startling statistic was when employees did not feel their manager focused on their strengths or positive characteristics, they were 71% "ACTIVELY disengaged."

The Society for Human Resource Management (SHRM) issued indicated in its 2016 Employee Job Satisfaction and Engagement report[iv] that was "very important" (between 46%-67%) that **management recognize employee job performance, provide respectful treatment and trust, and that supervisors respect for employees' ideas.**

For respectful treatment and trust between employees and management the generational gap was aligned; Baby Boomers, Generation X and Millennials all counted these in their top 5 crucial rankings. Those that may feel this is only a requirement for the younger generations have been proven incorrect in that assumption.

When we break down what respectful treatment and trust mean to people it includes being acknowledged and appreciated. When your teams feel trusted, empowered and the environment is safe and rewarding, then people thrive. They are a more positive, inter-connected group that better serves internal, and client facing end users and heightens employee productivity and wellness.

The Appreciative Inquiry approach is designed to focus less on negativity and criticism and instead utilize motivating incentives that encourage participation, innovation, and acceptance of change. Once again, it does not mean you ignore or dismiss employee performance improvement; you are merely using a more empowering "core behavioral change" perspective to address and lessen repeat situations. You have a focus on ensuring what the employee does well is not dismissed or overlooked.

Importantly, if a leader consistently chooses to focus on and address a person's "lack" areas without buffering that with attention to the positive aspects it doesn't take long for a person to feel demoralized and often stop caring about doing a good job. Why bother, it doesn't get rewarded.

Before you begin to utilize Appreciative Inquiry, let's explore what it is and what it means. It influences many communication techniques and practices. Learning this tool will not only benefit the employee but the entire company. It encourages more significant innovation, critical thinking, and team performance.

> *"I've learned that people will forget what you said,*
> *people will forget what you did,*
> *but people will never forget how you made them feel."*
> *~ Maya Angelou*

What is Appreciative Inquiry?

The most common definition of Appreciative Inquiry is *"the ability to recognize the best in people and utilizing those strengths to discover new possibilities and results."* The value is *"teams, organizations and society evolve in whatever direction we collectively, passionately and persistently ask questions about."*[v] It focuses on positive thinking and expresses ideas and opinions to reach an end-result.

What does that mean for you or your business? At its most basic level, this encourages employees to think positively about their value to the organization. This, in turn, helps them to overcome their own negative thought cycles, increases efforts to work towards and reach their personal goals for better productivity.

With a global perspective influencing all businesses these days, it means having leadership and employee mindset of positivity in critical thinking. This will aid innovation and creative problem solving as your organization evolves. In my experience, a person who feels appreciated will always do more than expected.

*It could be argued that all leadership is
appreciative leadership.
It's the capacity to see the best in the world around us, in our
colleagues, and in the groups, we are trying to lead.*

*~ David Cooperrider, Professor in Appreciative Inquiry,
and Faculty Director*

CHAPTER 3

LEADING A POSITIVE CULTURE

If your actions inspire others to dream more, learn more, do more and become more, you are a leader.
~John Quincy Adams

How does Appreciative Inquiry help build employee engagement and positive culture? By utilizing questions to adjust a person's focus on their past, present, and future successes. These questions will generally focus on what the person likes about their environment and the current situation. This enables the individual to take pride and comfort in what is going well.

With the positive identified, the person is more apt to consider and self-identify where they need to focus on for improvement and look forward to building momentum for success. Since we learn from our past mistakes and choices, we can use the questions asked to come up with insights, own them and identify them in our internal language.

This skill develops an ability to learn from past experiences and make better decisions and choices in the future. We are better able to understand where improvements can be made without defensiveness and to design an action plan for development that makes sense to our thought process and personality style.

The objective is identifying what works for you, and how you can use this knowledge to your advantage to create a better future then coaching your team to do the same. Leading with expertise means developing and guiding your own inner Appreciative Inquiry dialogue.

1. **Determine your goals, set objectives and a timeline.**

2. **Create a set of positive inquiry questions that will move you forward in achieving your goals.**

3. **Set aside time to ask yourself your Appreciative Inquiry questions and stop any negative interference with "I am not focusing on what was missed, only what was achieved at this time," and continue to document the positive.**

4. **Once you have gone through your series of questions, ask what needs to be done to continue to move productively towards an objective.**

EXAMPLE:

Overall Goal: I want to be more productive.

Objective: "I want to block time in my work calendar reviewing material, so I am better prepared for meetings."

Appreciative Inquiry Questions:

- *Did I block time on my calendar to meet my objective?*

- *What did I like most about this new way we are preparing for meetings?*

- *Is there a better way to reach this objective?*

- *What steps should I take to achieve a better way to meet this objective?*

Your review may be that you blocked time. However, it was regularly interrupted. Therefore, you need to review and decide on a better time, better ways to prevent interruptions or to break into smaller chunks of review time, etc. The idea being the focus is not what did not work and giving up effort on the objective, it is finding a better way to accomplish it.

Engaging People in Positive Thought

One of the age-old ways to determine how a person views a situation is to ask if the glass is half full or half empty. Many pessimists will reply that the glass is half empty while an optimist will see the glass as half full.

Even one pessimist in the group can hinder others "innovative ideas attitude." It is important to engage every employee and set an expectation of positive contribution. It creates a more pleasant work environment for everyone, and employees begin to feel more comfortable about sharing ideas and feeling increased pride in accomplishments, which influences greater productivity.

Your negative nellies have a place in identifying risks so long as they do so with a mindset of presenting contingent options and ideas for overcoming the hindering issue.

Consider it on a strategic level; at some point, your business objectives will need to adapt, change, or evolve. Developing your team's ability to engage in "think tank methodology" for smaller issues builds their skillset and resilience for larger changes that may be coming. Doing so with positive framing pushes mindsets towards innovative thinking and away from "but we've always done it this way," a form of comfort zone stagnation.

This exercise isn't recommended for every aspect of work, but it is a great way to brainstorm changes while developing your team's involvement and acceptance of new technology and business goals.

Brainstorming

Encourage group discussions in a controlled manner, one idea per person; no theories are considered wrong or "dumb." In a rotation, everyone takes a turn, one idea at a time. This avoids the personality that takes over discussions or talks down others' opinions.

Invite the team to comment on the ideas and opinions shared in the same roundtable format to grow and develop the suggestions provided. Establish the rule that only a positive framing is to be used to describe or add to any idea; negative phrasings are to be avoided.

For example, rather than "that is too risky to do," teach the wording "we should take the time to identify risks and plan contingencies on that idea."

I always made this fun, the team agreed to using a buzzer or bell to catch negativity. Each team member took turns playing the "buzz kill" moderator allowing some entertainment into the process of transforming your team. If your organization is more conservative having a meeting moderator raise a hand and ask for the idea or thought to be reframed also works well.

Behavior change takes consistency though. If you begin this process, make sure that every member is aware of what the objective is; why you are doing it; and include them in the assessment design, validation process and implementation planning.

Change the Person, Change the Organization

When employees take pride in themselves, in their ideas, in building a better team, they also take pride in their company. When they have negative feelings about where they work, it will show in their productivity and how they interact with others, including your customer base, whether internal or external.

When you change how a person views or thinks about the company, their team, and their contribution to it, you, in turn, improve how the company is perceived as a whole.

The internet has opened up the ability of an employee to "vent" as well as provide "accolades" for their organization, and the fact is, your customers and the public are watching. How do you wish your employees to represent your brand?

We know feedback influences our customer base, but a growing trend is company and management ratings on recruitment sites, which impacts the pool of talent you are enticing. Glassdoor, a recruitment site with 32 million monthly users, shared a survey[vi] indicating:

> ***"Fewer than half (49%) of employees would recommend their employer to a friend."***

With increasing numbers, people are adding ratings and comments on companies they are currently employed at or have worked for. This is quite eye opening given another publication shared that most job seekers are reviewing this feedback and commentary during their search.

The culture of your company is not only informed by what you design on your websites with marketing firms. Potential candidates are getting an inside view even if they don't know anyone within and that can impact top talent from wanting to apply. Employees are now brand ambassadors and recruitment marketers for your organization.

> ***"87% of Glassdoor users find the employer perspective useful when learning about jobs and companies."[vii]***

Since its inception in 1980 Appreciative Inquiry has grown and *"evolved from a theory to a practical process for positive change management in organizations."*

A Deloitte article[viii] states:

> ***"Culture and engagement are the most important issue companies face around the world. 87 percent of organizations cite culture and engagement as one of their top challenges, and 50 percent call the problem "very important."***

This statistic informs us of why it is so essential to meet with employees and listen to what they have to say; to value their ideas and opinions and open yourself to the type of learning and development that will positively transform your team. With confident, innovative, and reflective employees, led by management that appreciates them, your company gains a stronger change in an adaptive culture. This positive environment will reflect in the service provided internally and externally, and that can have a dramatic impact on the bottom line. It will also serve you well when you are ready to recruit and bring onboard new staff.

Employees seek a positive workplace culture, one that affirms that they are making a valued contribution to the company. They want to understand the alignment from the strategic vision to the departmental objectives to how their role is supporting the overall organization. With this clarity, they feel more inclined to think positively about their overall view of the organization and their purpose within a team.

An aspect of maintaining engaged, productive teams is ensuring they are part of any change initiative early on in the planning stage. My roles within corporations often provided me with a seat at the executive table during planning functions.

I cannot count the times I would need to vigorously advocate to communicate and inform employees at every level of ongoing information and allow a process of input from every level about what we were undertaking. The value in contribution from all known and potential stakeholders and end users to aid proper planning and not impede progress is critical. Employees have experience and information that can offer significant insight into any change initiative.

Psychologically, when they are aware early on, they are more apt to accept change positively, especially when they are included in the planning process. Beyond change initiatives too, it equally applies to better strategic planning all the way through to individual work plan development.

I will mention our Team Building workshop as it has proven to be a highly useful starting point for many organizations. If you have made it to the end of this chapter and cannot see your workgroup or organization adopting an Appreciative Inquiry mindset, then I suggest we start a conversation to build a stronger team foundation.

We adapt the content of this core program with a needs analysis that identifies where teams are currently at in employee engagement and leadership development. We then create measurable indicators to show the advancing results. If desired, we design hour-long follow-up training based on the timed feedback as your team progresses and coaching segments for leaders.

We have received incredible accolades from all types of organizations and professions on how our training makes a considerable and impactful difference to teams, client interactions and inter-departmental relationships. Please, check out some testimonials at www.DvKPartnerGroup.com.

The most personally satisfying feedback our training teams receive is how much the core program information helps attendees' personal lives and the moments that matter most." This result overflows nicely into the workplace. Enhancing overall wellness through increased emotional intelligence and stress reduction techniques is a fantastic benefit. This isn't just another workshop, it's a way of being that works in all aspects of your life, so it sticks! If you have teams that are in the forming stage, disengaged, or toxic this is a compelling new direction.

Training that positively impacts an employee's personal life only bodes well for an organization. Employee wellness can have a significant impact on team effectiveness, and the budget, but it is not entirely within an organization's control. When you provide training that impacts and improves individuals off hours significantly it only enhances the results you get on the job. Author, James MacNeil sums it up nicely with this following quote.

"Well people treat others well; hurt people, tend to hurt others. Drowning people tend to be insensitive"
                ~ James MacNeil

CHAPTER 4

TO THINK IS TO BE

*Whether you think you can, or,
whether you think you can't.
You're usually right.
~Henry Ford*

One of the simplest ways to feel more positive, confident, and self-assured is to alter the way we think about situations in our lives. When we have developed strong Emotional Intelligence, a positive, healthier attitude flows, which allows you to change your path to success.

Part of Emotional Intelligence is having a healthy, resilient mindset. It empowers you by giving you a heightened awareness of how you fit into your surroundings. It also builds the confidence required to use your strengths and expertise to your advantage, which develops comfort with change and builds adaptability.

Change, the only constant, is the birthplace of innovation. Embracing this fact will improve a person's resilience in all aspects of life. An essential mindset in a world that is not standing still, slowing down or moving backwards. How we adapt to the evolution of life is key to both our success and wellness.

As a leader, you are expected to make change happen with positive results. As an impacted person, your continued success and wellness, beginning with stress, can be dramatically affected by your attitude towards change. When we hide behind negative thoughts and allow our environment to make us sad or depressed, we may never have the drive to try new things or reach our goals and ambitions.

There is contagious power in groupthink. When one member of a team is adopting a negative resistance to a change or starts rallying behind the "change fatigue" mindset, it can catch on fast. Also, if a few leaders are also disengaged in a change process, then malcontent is inflamed even quicker, which can be very damaging to an organization. From costly, slow execution to maladaptive efforts to block and hinder progress.

Good leaders show the way by encouraging all and being supportive of change ambassadors and their objectives to build positive momentum towards a future state. A goal is more achievable when workgroups are engaged and actively appreciated for their contributions to the change.

As I noted earlier, the communication strategy of Appreciative Inquiry is a foundational one that aids change and transitions within your team when they arise. Therefore, beginning with your leadership group and flowing through your organization, a culture of positive thinking needs to be cultivated and encouraged.

Shift from a "*What's Wrong*" perspective to a "*What's Right*"?

It is difficult to tap into a positive, forward-thinking mindset when concentrating on a view of a situation from the negative aspects, or the "what's wrong" perspective. If there are impacting negatives, you will need to address them. However, there is a difference between being bogged down in the negatives aspects and seeking opportunity by reviewing the negatives as challenges or risks with the intent to find solutions. Positive framing opens up the mind.

One of my most popular Project Leadership seminars is "Failing Forward; seeking excellence in Project Management one unique mistake at a time." A good leader or change ambassador knows that the very idea of something "new" means we do not have all the answers up front, the very definition of a project states it is a "unique endeavor." The full definition of a Project per PMI[ix] **"a project is a temporary endeavor undertaken to create a unique product, service or result."**

A project manager's starting point needs to be with an open, positive, humble respect that it hasn't been done exactly the same way before and a positive team mindset will be required to be most successful. This is why planning is such a crucial stage, and needs people input, from a well thought out, broad stakeholder group.

Often planning is done quickly, with too few people and with a focus too ingrained in scope, budget, and time frame from the negative "what could go wrong" mentality, forgetting to consider what could go right with robust people involvement and a creative, well-considered, change management and communication plan.

I would often lead planning sessions by stating, *"we never have enough time to plan a project thoroughly, yet we always seem to find the time to revise, re-do and delay a project when it is not planned well,"* so let's focus on doing this right the first time.

My years of being tasked to recover crashing projects or mentor leaders of failing projects identified repetitive situations. These seemed to correlate with the issues I discovered when being asked to take over a "troubled" workgroup in Operations or Client Services. The top three pain points were poor communication strategies, deficient change management planning and ineffective engagement, whether with stakeholders, customers, or employees.

Change initiatives are very similar. If market trends, mergers, technological innovations, politics, or laws, to name a few, are moving us in new directions then it is precisely that: "new," and it is possible not every single aspect will be thought out in advance or executed without complications. Knowing that and building in adaptability and evolution phases gives you a significant advantage. Sufficiently communicating that as a known factor to your employees lays the groundwork, so they are prepared for change and an agile implementation. When you make them part of the process, then you are a superstar leader.

Reviewing "lessons learned" from similar projects is an excellent tool for an organization to refer to in the planning. Many managers tend to shy away from pointing out perceived errors in previous work, either for concern they are critiquing someone else's output or just not seeing the value in the process. However, the most effective planning process includes robust people input. The stakeholders touched by the changes and all those implementing or impacted by anything new as well as those who participated in a previous similar project.

Using the Appreciative Inquiry method lessens the potential "sting" or perception of negativity from lessons learned in the past. Question those involved with a discovery mindset that shows you are curious to learn from them. It shows their thoughts and opinions count and engages them in the new project or initiative.

- **What did they like the most?**
- **What went well?**
- **What could have used some tweaking along the way?**
- **What was missed, overlooked or not efficient in the process?**

When these are asked in a respectful, information seeking manner that balances positive and negative input, folks are happy to oblige. For the future change initiatives use the same technique with a positive framing.

- **What would be the ideal state?**

- **Where do you foresee stumbling blocks along the way and how would you suggest handling them?**

- **What do you feel might inhibit a successful change, and why?**

You can see how this creates active and positive involvement. Employees have an awareness that something is coming which lessens the fear of change because they were involved, listened to, respected and part of the planning process. Having the people currently doing similar work and those that will be impacted by the change involved early on will aid the planning process immensely.

Delegating change ambassadors from that group to lead the discussions provides empowerment that will resonate with your whole team. They will be more engaged, as part of the change, and influencing the process, not just impacted by it. You will be very impressed with how this one action can affect the percentage split of engaged vs resistant and lessen the power of those opposed.

When I was approving the stage gates (proceed or stop moments in a project) of a Project Manager's work the most challenging task was teaching them that understanding why they should identify and proactively seek out the failure or weak points, in a positive manner, was a good thing.

With Appreciative Inquiry questioning techniques, you can communicate you care about the best results. By identifying what went well, what needed some refocusing and what needed to be avoided or done better next time, you now have the insight to adapt and manage the next stage in a more controlled and efficient manner.

This technique gives people confidence that you seek and accept their expertise, opinions, and insight. When you respect and expect the best out of others, they often step up! The same applies to operational reviews, strategic planning, and innovation; the negative aspects need to be considered and potential fail points identified for contingency planning. This approach remains positively focused, inclusive, and respectful with the aim that adapting, evolving and healthy growth is the targeted outcome for everyone in the organization.

Beginning with the positive and only defining potential negatives as steppingstones to a better way you empower yourself and your team to think about an improved future state first. You move away from getting pulled down and stuck mulling over the negatives, trying to assign blame, or convincing yourselves that something will never work. You'll find that any situation won't appear as bad as you think when you notice the positive first. Then move to the maybe's and then tackle the negatives with an aim to change them.

Providing guidance towards improved outcomes can be a sensitive part of a leader's job. Used consistently, Appreciative Inquiry eases the challenge significantly and remains as critical in Operations, Customer Service, Employee Engagement and Leadership Development as it does in Project Management. When people see improvement as a positive and forward-thinking part of their contribution, at any level, they embrace change and transformation better, and you are not dealing with the same level of evasiveness or defensiveness anymore.

Since the primary purpose of this tool is positivity-based leadership for enhanced engagement through a goal-oriented focus, a pessimistic attitude won't get anyone very far.
If that is your norm, this will take some practice. You will have problems presented to you; this is just changing the process of how you look at them. Take a few minutes and look at all sides of the issue starting with the most favorable aspect or potential opportunity.

Using what is great, what is good, what could use some tweaking or improvement before moving to what needs some targeted focus is a helpful step by step process to see a holistic view of any situation.

One of my favorite project sayings was "if I am the smartest person in this room, there's a problem." Which does not stem from a lack of confidence in my intelligence or expertise; I am merely comfortable with the knowledge I only know what I know, I am an expert in some areas and a new learner in others.

As a leader, if I have not chosen to surround myself with people that can offer different perspectives and expertise, then I am not as bright as I think I am. If this is not your mindset, consider adopting it.

If you find yourself getting stuck in the negative muck, you need to reach out to other impacted people and areas and ask THEM to help assess your plan to avoid a limited or biased perspective. Often these different inputs will calm any uncertainty and broaden your view significantly.

You now know how valuable your team is in making transformational change happen and solving problems that will enhance employee engagement, client service or profit, so get them involved! Asking your team to be part of any planning process or operational review values their expertise and builds a positive, innovative atmosphere. When you genuinely care to hear what they have to say and offer, you are on your way to being an exceptional leader.

Keys to shifting away from a negative mindset

Avoid the "all or nothing" thinking, determining that a situation only has two sides is limiting. Most cases are not that simplistic. Think about a prism with shooting beams that impacts far and wide; this is more apt to be the reality.

Recognize there is an impactful difference between always being right and having a happy and "well" engaged team. Some leaders think that by their title they have to know all the answers; leadership is not a solo act.

Develop a mindset of *"I only know what I know right now,"* remain open to learning and discovering; you will be far more effective and able to maintain positive framing.

Avoid over-generalizing a situation; focus on details should this happen. By breaking it down into smaller bits, you can see how each segment is impactful from a positive to a potential negative and you can lessen emotion towards any perceived problem. With an Adult Ego State, it is much easier to manage; we will learn more about that later. List out your perceptions and biased opinions and research all possible variables. It helps put variety and options on the table for your consideration.

The Johari Window

A useful model to share with your employees to build their openness to learning new things and embracing change is Dr. Joseph Luft, and Dr. Harry Ingram's Johari Window. This model allows a greater understanding of self, as well as a greater understanding of others. It helps open people up to learning and reevaluating previous perceptions and bias. It further leads the way to better team dynamics between different areas of expertise and across cultural divides. It's Not Eliminating Mistakes; It's Building Up Successes

- Open area: All information that I know about myself, and the information others know of me, possibly disclosed, or observed.

- Blind spot: Things that others see in me, but I am unaware of myself.

- Hidden area: The things that I know about myself, but others do not know about me.

- Unknown area: This includes everything that I do not know about myself, and you do not know about me.

Johari Window

	Known to self	Not known to self
Known to others	Arena	Blind spot
Not known to others	Façade	Unknown

One common misconception that people make is that being positive or using these tactics means they cannot address mistakes or find faults. Naturally, everything is not puppies, kittens, and rainbows all the time, this is not the intent of Appreciative Inquiry.

Mistakes, errors, oversights, and mishaps happen all the time, and while they are preventable at times, they cannot be stopped altogether. The key is to understand that mistakes are a growth tool, an opportunity to learn from and aid your future successes. That we all make mistakes is a given; it's how we manage them, productively and helpfully, that is the key to success. How do we define a lesson from them in a manner that builds on our development progress?

Consider a mistake that you have learned from in the past. There will be many in your life you can choose whether through your own experience or watching others. What did the mistake teach you?

Still hard on yourself and others? Read the following and then think about that mistake again, in a new light. Give yourself some grace while determining what you could have learned, or can still learn, with this new perspective.

> *You are watching a child learn to ride their bicycle for the first time. Seeing their eager face and feeling their hyped-up excitement to get it right.*
>
> *They fail the first few times, but either right away or after a pause and a hug, they go for it once more.*
>
> *You can feel their concentration, reviewing what they have tried and taking in the new information from those around them all in their effort to gain the right balance.*
>
> *Suddenly, they get it! A with a whoop of excitement they are on their own, wind in their hair and maintaining their balance.*

In your mind, are you cheering them on? Offering advice and tips? Running alongside them to give them some comfort if they falter? We often forget to analyze our learnings and all the insights and tips and experiences that formed how we ended up doing better and those that helped us along the way. Rarely did we get very good at anything without some teaching, coaching, mentoring or guidance from another.

When viewing that scenario in your mind did you focus your thoughts on how many times they fell? Was there anyone else in your mind watching too, parents, relatives, neighbors? Were they cheering and offering advice or labelling the child a failure and giving up on them?

I would expect that most folks are cheering and offering advice. Recognizing that the child is learning something they didn't know before and giving the appropriate grace and acceptance to the new effort.

Again, I don't wish to suggest you can do something blatantly wrong and say, "well, I didn't know" expecting to be cheered on to do better next time. This exercise is about framing your mindset internally and giving yourself the ability to see the positive aspects first. A focus on learning from and doing better and reaching a handout to those who are also learning how to build their expertise.

Being positive doesn't mean we eliminate mistakes or problems. We accept them as part of the learning process and where possible plan contingencies for when they happen. We adapt and overcome by having a primary focus on the outcome desired and the achievements we aim for along the way. Success will lead to more success when we prioritize our attention on the positive.

"Appreciation is a wonderful thing.
It makes what is excellent in others belong to us as well."
~Voltaire

CHAPTER 5

THE POWER OF WORDS

*Appreciation can make a day; even change a life.
Your willingness to put it into words
is all that is necessary.
~Margaret Cousins*

Why does the "power of words" have such a significant impact on us? Consider your youth; do you recall being more invigorated by positive language than negative? The psychology of using *"don't, can't, won't"* is well documented as damaging to our brains. In Psychology Today[x], Andrew Newberg, M.D. and Mark Waldman give us a clear summary of the power of no.

They write about the results from a neural MRI scan that videos changes in our brains as the word "NO" flashes for less than a second. Findings show a "sudden release of dozens of stress-producing hormones as well as neurotransmitters. These chemicals immediately interrupt the normal functioning of your brain, impairing logic, reason, language processing, and communication."

They further explain that exposure to negative words will make a *"highly anxious or depressed person" feel worse after, and the more you ruminate on negative words, the more you can damage key structures that regulate your memory, feelings, and emotions."*

Imagine how this may impact your workplace teams when negative personnel are left unmanaged or toxic bosses and employees are left unchecked. I believe leadership has an obligation to create a positive, healthy workplace.

Wellbeing is further impaired when you vocalize your negativity, or even slightly frown when you're talking. This causes more stress chemicals to be released, not only in your brain, but your listener's brain as well. *"The listener will experience increased anxiety and irritability, thus undermining cooperation and trust. In fact, just hanging around negative people will make you more negative toward others!"* This is why some people have the capability to drain us emotionally.

Scientifically, this is very telling on how toxic or poisonous work environments become very disruptive. Consider the influence of both the subconscious and conscious mind absorbing the environment it is exposed to for any significant amount of time and the impact it can have on team positivity or toxicity. It goes deeper than external communications, as it starts with the inner voice. A team low in Emotional Intelligence will also be more inclined to be beating themselves up on the inside. A combination of low EI and negative communication norms will not engage, motivate, and drive a high-performing team.

Envision the last time you were in a lousy mood and hung out with friends who were having a great time, laughing, and enjoying life. How long did it take for your spirit to shift? Conversely, think of a time when someone entered the room with a nasty mood that negatively impacted you.

That employee or group, or boss, that is continuously offering negative commentary or bullying others will get into your mind and settle in if you let it. If you begin to mull over those same thoughts, you may change your thinking, and potentially you may show behavior changes for the worse.

Even if you do not repeat them within yourself, there is emotional contagion felt from those who do. It's called the Open Loop Limbic System, and it picks up on the resonance or vibe of the people around you. For self-development, we need to understand that the power of our subconscious is quite good at giving us exactly what we input.

In the book, Primal Leadership, by authors Goleman, Boyatzis, and McKee the open-loop phenomenon defines how emotions spread like a contagion between people. There is a study cited where scientists measure the heart rate of two people as they have a good conversation. At the beginning of the conversation, their bodies are functioning at different rhythms, but fifteen minutes later their physiological profiles look remarkably similar, what is called mirroring.

The Scientists described the limbic loop as an *"interpersonal limbic regulation,"* when one person transmits signals that can alter hormone levels, cardiovascular function, sleep rhythms, and even immune function inside the body of someone else. The open-loop limbic system means that other people have the power to change our physiology and in turn that affects our emotions. A closed-loop system is self-regulating, therefore when we tell ourselves *"I can't do that"* or *"I'll never finish this"* we usually find ourselves to be absolutely right.

Our brains cannot compute the mass of possibilities opposite to our statement. The subconscious isn't designed to dispute you, so it will default to making what you input the outcome.

The basic concept and the easiest way to understand is to consider your brain a computer, a supercomputer at that! Your subconscious will only perform the tasks you program it to undertake. These *inputs* can impact both your psychological and physiological responses. The supercomputer is preloaded with biases, perceptions and beliefs that sit there in the background until you update the "software" with new information. Until you consciously decide to control the inputs, it is just humming along in the background with whatever old program is there.

The inputs to your subconscious programming come as you frame them or as you heard and accepted them on your life's journey, starting as a baby. The subconscious brain is merely recording, without fact checking or challenging the data. The programmer, YOU, your cognitive brain has the power of conscious choice on what you will input into the supercomputer. Your choice of input is the only controllable source.

When we use more positive and influential phrasing and language, in time, our new programming takes effect, and we become more confident and ready to handle any situation. This is the physiological response to the new data received. Our subconscious takes up the query and creates possibilities for us. Some of you may relate this to the Law of Attraction. Remember Open Loop Limbic System picks up on the resonance or vibe of the people around you, and they pick up on yours, *"like attracts like."*

Positive phrasing instructs your subconscious to seek solutions and "output" ideas and possibilities that resolve the query received. Consider some of the following and test it out for a week or two, you will feel the difference of positive over negative framing.

Simply add your desired outcome to:

- **"I can…"**
- **"I'm willing to …"**
- **"I will come up with the resolution to …"**
- **"I'm making progress on …"**
- **"I am in control of …"**
- **"I'm excellent at …"**

In my business, my favorite question is *"I want to know the best way to make "X" happen, feed me all the possibilities"* and let my subconscious feed me ideas or prompt me to ask the right questions of someone who has the answer I seek.

People have been amazed at how quickly solutions and ideas come to me, and it is not that I have expertise in the area explored, I love asking questions, getting broad perspectives from others, and then I expect my brain to come up with answers, so it does.

The Open Loop Limbic System proves that our thoughts and words are contagious. Share this concept with others and encourage them to think more positively too, both externally and internally! There are some who brighten a room when they enter it and others that bring a cloud of doom and gloom. No one wants to knowingly be the person that brightens the room best when they leave. Knowing you are now emotionally contagious practice being the person who lifts the spirit and enjoyment of a place, and you will feel the energy coming back to you.

Using Positive Language

Avoid negative phrasing containing such words as *"can't"* or *"won't."* Frame it, so you are seeking a positive solution or output. Be kind to yourself, remind yourself of your abilities and strengths. You are the programmer of your brain; it acts on your conscious command, so be a commanding leader worth listening to, every time. Compliment yourself, *"Good job"* and *"Well done."* You should work hardest to meet your own personal standard of good work, challenge yourself against beating your records and accomplishments.

Compliment others and be very specific about it! When you show you appreciate the little things your teammates do you will begin to notice it comes back to you and spreads amongst others as well. Creating an environment of appreciation and acceptance goes a long way to a happier life at work. Even outside of work, practice finding the good, attractive, and interesting in others.

When I meet someone, I look for something I like in them. Even those who are not necessarily pleasant will have something likable if you look hard enough. It becomes a practice of positivity that creates habits and mannerisms that translate back into your work life and thereby being a confident, motivating, encouraging leader becomes second nature. It also becomes clearly authentic. People can read you better than you may think (lots more on that in my body language workshop). I believe being authentic is imperative as a leader.

Limit or Remove Negative Phrasing

Positive phrasing impacts your thinking. The same goes for negative wording; when we allow ourselves to use negative language, our programmed responses become negative. Without changing the input programming, you are actively resisting and shutting down possibilities that aid a desired positive outcome. It will be much harder to accept change, feel empowered, change behaviors, achieve more, or transform yourself into better versions of you.

Studies have shown that there are certain phrases that any person should remove from their vocabulary to ban negative language. The top five are key to identify and remove from your vocabulary expediently. They are listed in the next pages.

*If you are a master at beating yourself up, you are the
master of holding yourself back.
~Deirdre von Krauskopf*

JUST

This word limits our accomplishments and devalues our skills. By saying phrases such as:

"I'm just a _____" or, "I just work in _____"

Limiting our worth can make anyone feel undervalued in their job. Every job relies on another to be successful, every role important to the overall success of a company. Begin instead to say, **"My contribution allows for "x" to happen" and recognize the value you bring.**

I learned this in the Military; every role had an impacting outcome on another. A well-oiled machine needs many parts working in tandem. I led this way early on at my first career job in the hospitality field, with staff housekeeping feeling they were not as valued as front desk clerks as an example. It only took a few weeks of teaching both sides that if we didn't have staff cleaning the rooms, we would have nothing to sell. If front desk staff didn't listen to the needs of clients from the housekeeping perspective, they would be handling more complaints.

Further, the housekeeping team was in the perfect position to converse with our customers, make a note of what they liked and didn't like. What they asked for most and what toiletries were used or ignored which I started feeding into our inventory and cost decisions. When they started believing in their worth, the positive comment cards jumped significantly. Which led to more rewards and recognition, happier teams, and better inter-departmental co-operation.

TRY

This word is a crutch used to avoid or delay saying no, or as an excuse to fail. We will *"try"* to accomplish something. It is like programming your brain's computer with a *"meh"* or shrug. You have clearly clarified it isn't essential and no real effort or commitment is required. When we don't want to succeed, then our brain is ready with an excuse or reason why it's not our fault. We either do something, or we don't.

Consider the words *"try"* and *"trying"* as expecting failure built into them, they weaken you and make you appear less confident. The idea speaks to more effort required as you are dragging your feet getting it done. If you feel a *"try"* about to slip from your lips, catch yourself and replace with definitive phrases, such as:

"I will try and get that report"	*"I am in the process of getting that report done."*
"I am trying to get into "x"	*"I am working towards getting into "x"*
"Try to understand"	*"I will explain where I am coming from, if you have questions, please ask."*

When you state you are *"going to"* do something, you have committed to an intention; it has an expectation of determination. Try is like *"maybe"* or *"I don't know"* these words are not driving results. We choose to commit, or we don't. To quote a famous but powerful movie phrase:

"Do. Or do not. There is no try."
~ Yoda (Star Wars)

CAN'T

This word is like giving up before considering possibilities and most likely to be used when we don't wish to make an effort to reach a goal or accomplishment, or we do not like the idea. It may be instigated by fear of the unknown or unwillingness to be vulnerable. Positive and honest reframes would include:

- *"I haven't learned how to do that yet."*
- *"I haven't given that any attention thus far."*
- *"That doesn't appeal to me at this time."*

Each of these is more truthful and real to yourself and others. It stops the impossibility factor and makes it a simple fact that will or will not be fulfilled.

Halfway through University my son was upset he didn't choose more sciences in high school. He wanted to change to a Marine Biologist and didn't have the prerequisites for that University program. When he said, *"I can't"* I corrected to *"he could"* but it would mean lots of studying and a delayed degree. So, the real issue was *"how badly did he want to make this change?"*

That is true of many of our *"I can't"* rants. There is an effort in change, and that is often the actual stumbling block. If you have no interest in learning or doing the task or situation presented to you then be honest to yourself and others.

- *"I will not be taking that direction at this time,"* or
- *"I won't be learning that any time soon,"* or
- *"I am not doing that."* Or *"I am not doing that yet."*

IMPOSSIBLE

In a business setting, this word is typically used when faced with something big and overwhelming. However, if broken down into smaller step by step segments or by seeking the right help a reasonable momentum can be expected. Perhaps it needs more time, a broader perspective, or external change first. It could require more resources or budget. It may be improbable, but few work tasks are genuinely *"impossible."*

During my time as a Project Portfolio Manager, my role included high value, politically sensitive, or high-risk, projects to manage directly or indirectly. If a project was failing, I was often tasked to step in and take a more prominent role in another's area as the Project Recovery Specialist. If I had started announcing it was impossible to manage these millions worth of projects, my tenor would have been cut short.

My prioritization skills were critical. At times I would need to negotiate with executive sponsors by asking, *"what would you like me to defer in order to make this" happen?"* If the answer was nothing then it was *"alright, so what budget or resources are you redirecting to me to ensure all projects continue on the current schedule?"* The goal is to help them understand the complexities of the workload from a big picture was vital. I had to be very open and transparent on what was required via resources, time, budget, or scope adjustment to manage the workload, without letting any balls drop. Take *"impossible"* and frame it as *"what would be needed to make this happen?"*

SOMEDAY

Similar to the word *"try"* this word sets us up to allow and almost expect failure. Physiologically and psychologically, it is a mental shrug or *"who cares."* If we tell ourselves we will start something or reach our goals *"someday,"* we are permitting ourselves to procrastinate and drop the ball. *"Someday"* is telling our supercomputer brain that this is the lowest of priorities and unimportant.

Be honest with yourself, admit it isn't a priority and assess whether it should be done at all. Allow yourself to be more mindful of the reasons why it is a someday issue in your mind. Perhaps it is merely something you want to *"go away"* where a straightforward word, *"no"* is the best answer. If it's simply a low priority, then defer it and list it in the decide box then add a date to it.

The Eisenhower Box

"What is important is seldom urgent, and what is urgent is seldom important"
~ Dwight Eisenhower, 34th President of the United States

	URGENT	NOT URGENT
IMPORTANT	DO Do it now!	DECIDE Schedule a time to complete it.
NOT IMPORTANT	DELEGATE Who can do it for you?	DELETE Eliminate it!

This is a time management tool created in many forms from an Eisenhower's speech. Coined the Eisenhower Productivity box, it is a great decision-making tool that will keep you on task!

Example:

Patricia was angry that her manager gave her another complex project to complete. *"Why me! Didn't he see how many mistakes I had made the last time?"* She became more and more frustrated as she drafted a rough project plan believing she didn't have enough time to finish by his due date and would have to turn it in very late. Patricia was ready to give up on the whole thing and quit.

When she spoke to her manager again, she blurted out how impossible the project was. He listened to her concerns and acknowledged they should review it. He started by saying that she always did a great job and that he had faith that she could complete this project successfully. It was why he chose her to lead it.

He then began asking her a series of questions about the tasks required, the timelines she had arrived at, what could be moved from her regular duties to achieve her plan and what help she would need to meet the project goals. By focusing on the positive aspects of achievement, they could begin to create a manageable workload with the right resources.

Patricia felt a huge weight off her shoulders and immediately began to feel better about it. Realizing that with a positive focus on what was required so the project could be achieved, the whole situation was less daunting. Knowing she could work through the outline with her manager and seek the help and guidance she needed to succeed and that he respected her work and opinions, gave her increasing confidence.

She was able to start remembering and focusing on all the successes she had on the last project, the team collaboration that helped, and that she did do a great job. She reviewed what went wrong during the previous project with a new light, using the lessons learned in her planning process to avoid duplication, which would save her a lot of time and effort.

When she turned in the final project on time, she realized her self-critical thinking almost got the best of her, and she needed to appreciate her planning strengths more.

*Whatever the mind can conceive and believe,
it can achieve.*
~Napoleon Hill

CHAPTER 6

NO MORE CHANGE FATIGUE!

Leaders in today's environment must create an adaptive change culture where one embraces business evolution as the new norm.
~ *Deirdre von Krauskopf*

Let's review how Appreciative Inquiry is aligned to our change culture. Globalization has been influencing how Human Resources and Leadership Executives manage the need for continuous development and the impact of constant change initiatives. Having an informed and knowledgeable staff is critical to meet the demands of a global and evolving customer base. These leaders also must ensure employees have the awareness and soft skills to manage across growing worldwide environments of diverse cultural norms and generational differences.

All this means creating processes and strategies to meet a flow of change, which is no longer a straightforward technological or operational adaptation every so often. Many organizations today are in a continual transformation mode. When this *"new norm"* is not managed well, it can lead to employee frustration or *"change fatigue."*

Not necessarily a new challenge but managing it well does require a dramatic shift in how organizations approach change processes and strategies. It also significantly impacts employee wellness, attendance, and teamwork.

The philosophy and integration of Appreciative Inquiry is a communications strategy to develop stronger team leaders. Initiated in the mid-80's when a graduate student from Case Western Reserve University, David Cooperrider, conducted an organizational review of the Cleveland Clinic.

In his research and observations, he concluded an unusually high level of cooperation and innovation within this particular organization. Cooperrider, with assistance from his student advisor, Suresh Srivastava, analyzed the factors that contributed to the functioning of the clinic at its best, those moments of exceptional performance. In 1987, they published a broadly distributed article *"Appreciative Inquiry in Organizational Life"* [xi] in Research in Organization. In it, they described the research, theory, and practice.

For over fifteen years after their publication, Cooperrider resisted requests to write a *"how to"* preferring that folks kept their focus on the principles of the model and championed widespread innovation in methods; therefore, many iterations are available. The initial paper outlined that it begins with appreciation, it is collaborative, it is provocative, and it needs to be applicable.

In time, Cooperrider and Diana Whitney published the five principles that are the primary citations which detail why appreciative inquiry questions lead to positive change in a paper titled *"Appreciative Inquiry: A Positive Revolution in Change"*[xii]

The Constructionist Principle proposes that what we believe to be true determines what we do and thought, and action emerge out of relationships.

- *In this, our daily conversations begin to morph the culture of an organization and certainly a workgroup. Negativity begets viral negativity, and conversely, positive framing shapes a more positive thinking environment. Appreciative Inquiry transforms to the latter and generates more innovative freedom and cooperative attitudes.*

The Simultaneity Principle proposes that as we inquire into human systems, we change them and the seeds of change, the things people think and talk about, what they discover and learn, are implicit in the very first questions asked.

- *Perhaps you can relate to an authority figure at some point in your life that always asked questions in a way that made you feel that no matter what you said you would be wrong or in trouble. Questioning techniques are significant; it is not a neutral tool. The manner of inquiry leads to the common understanding. If you are seeking answers to the negative you will get them; if seeking answers to a possibility, you will attain that outcome too.*

The Poetic Principle proposes that organizational life is expressed in the stories people tell each other every day, and the story of the organization is constantly being co-authored.

- *Our thoughts influence our actions, so if conversations are framed with an overarching negativity belief, then the words we choose will align with our thought process. A self-fulfilling prophecy begins to unfold if the unproductive and damaging sentiment remains unchallenged. Learning to train our thoughts to focus on developing the best version of others and ourselves allows internal culture shifts towards positivity that shine outward.*

The Anticipatory Principle postulates that what we do today is guided by our image of the future.

- *Similar to the self-fulfilling prophecy, neuroscience proves the incredible adaptability of the mind. The subconscious is wired to deliver based on your inputs. I delve into this in greater detail in all our training as it is so compelling. Imagine your subconscious providing exactly what you ask of it; it is entirely within your power. Your thoughts are being accepted as factual data, and the brain will put great effort in achieving the outcome of that input. When our teams are in a state of dysfunction only a consistent and planned infusion of positive thought would change the culture wiring that has formed.*

The Positive Principle proposes that momentum and sustainable change requires positive affect and social bonding.

- *This tool isn't a "one-off" attempt to make someone's day better. A consistent sentiment of inspiration, focusing on what went right and an openness to innovation, builds the momentum to a way of being within your organization. It also promotes strong connections and relationships between people, particularly between groups in conflict, required for collective inquiry and change.*

As leaders, you will find Appreciative Inquiry opens new doors for gaining cooperation and engagement with your teams as well as developing a new way of thinking that could impact other areas of your life. With positive thoughts and attitude among your group and yourself, you will discover new ways of reaching your goals and create a motivated environment more attuned to open and creative thinking.

The "4 D" Cycle of Appreciative Inquiry[xiii]

The 4D process to implement and maintain an Appreciative Inquiry workplace is an iterative, ongoing cycle consisting of four phases:

- Discovery
- Dream
- Design
- Delivery

This model gives you a process to follow for operational and employee performance planning. Personally, I have found it beneficial when both align well with the department plans and the strategic objectives of your organization. In my experience, this is not as common as you may think, and it causes a disconnection of purpose.

When your team knows what they are expected to achieve and are part of the process of building those goals, there is an increase in productivity and engagement. More importantly, for the wellness of your team, the commitment and understanding of a known and evolving future is more welcomed and accepted. This lessens the stress and disrupting elements that are the root of change fatigue.

The overview of the 4D model is:

Discovery

- Research, through collaborative questioning the most significant area(s) to evolve.

Dream

- Create your team's vision of an ideal future.

Design

- Develop objectives to create opportunities for the changes needed to arrive at your ideal future.

Delivery

- Share your intent, so the behavior change is not coming as a surprise and begin to implement your objectives consistently. Seek regular feedback and discover what is working well, what could use some tweaking and what is not coming across as authentic or raising the environment to one feeling more appreciated.

I prefer to include in another aspect, the "Do Over" as part of the delivery, as the environment can and will consistently change, so building in a component of review and renewal builds the expectation and acceptance of constant evolution.

Do Over

- As the process becomes more natural with your team, begin to expand your innovation objectives and empowerment strategies. Build learning objectives and stretch goals into your performance reviews and see where you can lead your team and the members that contribute to your organization's success.

"The secret of change is to focus all of your energy, not on fighting the old, but on building the new."
~Socrates

The gains to your team objectives become evident very quickly when all members feel included in the process of their improvement. Employees often discover gains in cooperation, within their workgroups, inter-departmentally and cross-departmentally, when they explore options and find out what was attempted and thought of before. All of this can lead employees to feel more appreciative of their role in the company and what they can do to make meaningful contributions.

From my feedback sessions over the years, I have found that some struggle with the idea of a "dream" phase. Think of it like this; the dream phase focuses on what "possibilities" would work for you and the company in the future.

This process is especially helpful when creating Strategic Plans at higher levels and department or workgroup plans. I have often led such planning sessions with "if there were no rules, policies or processes in place what do you envision is possible?"

This process will involve some *"pie in the sky"* thinking at the start. However, the underlying goal is break down barriers from; *"my ideas are stupid, or I'm not going to be heard because it is too different from our norm"* through to *"we can't change anything because of some policy or rule"* and *"that's the way its always been done."*

You are building a comfort for agile, adaptable, out of the box thinking. You will get to a stage where the unlikely ideas shift to a *"future cloud"* quickly while raising both the good humor and critical thinking involvement of your team; and then the real work begins. This tiny segment in a planning session has now opened the tap to a flow of creativity and innovation that would otherwise be dripping. The next roundtable of ideas will be ones that can be evaluated and streamlined through the subsequent stage discussions and feasibility reviews to achievable goals.

Surprisingly, there are times when some of those "parked" ideas also make their way into the planning. The ones that make sense to question for future change are now considered ideas for advocacy. Ideas that would change the barriers that would otherwise be left to that "we have always done it this way" stagnation that so many companies face. It can open up the path to real innovative possibilities and more importantly sets a framework of acceptability to change and innovation. Which, of course, serves the company well as they evolve with marketplace demand.

This *"dream session"* can be run in a large group conference or done with a few peers. Either way, it should allow everyone to open up about how they see their value and contribution to the company as it relates to the strategic plan and the operational plans.

The process also provides you with meaningful feedback along the way as you collect input for the next planning session and feed some of those *"pie in the sky ideas"* to the next tier leadership as the innovative possibilities YOUR engaged team produced.

*"Change your thoughts, and
you change your world."*
~Norman Vincent Peale

Question Examples:

- *"If our current policies and processes were completely flexible, what would you change?"*

- *"Do you see this as an immediate change or one to work towards in the future?"*

- *"What changes could "I" make in my daily role to be more impactful to our client/end user?"*

- *"If I could change one way that we do business what would be most beneficial to our team / the company?"*

- *"What, in these ideas, can we implement today to help reach our operational and strategic objectives?"*

- *"What considerations are needed from senior management to make the future vision happen?"*

Another important consideration for efficiently transforming your culture into an innovative and change responsive team is collaborative involvement. The more you involve your team, the more effective you will be.

Creating the design plan is all about how you and your team plan to reach the goals and objectives outlined in the discovery and dream phases. This part of the model focuses on what needs to be done to reach these goals and achieve the required progress. A genuine change responsive team does this together so that all are part of the creation of objectives and feel an ownership in the outcome due to that participation.

Where current state impedes a forward movement, you can move it to later discussions, dismiss them after consideration or brainstorm how you would advocate for or change the current state to allow the idea to be feasible. The group is encouraged to use positive language and invite their co-workers to think about possibilities, not roadblocks.

Examples:

- *"What do we need to do to make this happen?"*
- *"Will things need to be changed or altered?"*
- *"Do we need to introduce a new element?"*

By including your team in the design, they will be much more engaged in the delivery phase, the final stage of the 4-D model. In this part of the model, employees need to take the necessary actions to progress toward change and positively achieve the team goals. When the team is engaged in designing the operational plan, they have a much stronger buy-in.

A plan isn't worth the paper it is written on if it doesn't have an engaged, dynamic team behind it to carry it out. Part of the success can be achievable goals that are well celebrated to energize the positive mindset.

Do not miss the power of building in a *"Do-Over"* element to create an expectation that all aspects of the business are fluid and evolving to maintain a competitive and modern edge. You may also find that creating the ideology of being at the forefront of designing *"next practices"* not simply *"best practices"* builds the innovative mindset within your groups. This add-on to the model also significantly lessens the *"change fatigue"* feedback that can harm a well-functioning, cohesive and productive team.

From my early years of teaching Total Quality Management (TQM), I have mentored others to build this agile type of methodology of continual renewal into the planning. In my opinion, it should be evident in all procedures, policies, processes, and performance plans.

Tasks

- **Implement any changes needed**
- **Remove elements that no longer work**
- **Assign responsibilities and duties as required**
- **Celebrate wins and successes, even the small ones**
- **Build expectations for the next iteration**

Practical Illustration

Jeremy was working with a group of employees who were creating a new form of marketing for the company. Many of them had run out of ideas and weren't sure where to start.

Jeremy asked the employees what they noticed had worked for the company in the past. Everyone named several methods that had been successful. Then he did a round of their favorite marketing from different companies. What was it about that excited them both?

Then he asked them, without any of the barriers that may be in their current situation, what could they think of to create improvements? With the open freedom to ideas, what did they wish to see for the marketing scheme? How could this out-of-box framing boost the companies brand?

He wanted them to imagine the big picture and tap into their innovative minds. Then he asked them to come up with one action that would get them to that success.

He asked them what resources and items they would need to get there. Several employees displayed their new ideas, each played off one another, creating an exciting and innovative plan.

Jeremy told them the last thing they needed to do was put those ideas into action. That was their next big step.

"Change is the law of life and those who look only to the past or present are certain to miss the future."

~John F. Kennedy

CHAPTER 7

ON-BOARDING SPECIAL SAUCE

If not critical for the specialty of the roll, hire for attitude and transferable skills over specific experience. Behavior predicts behavior; tasks can be learned.
~Deirdre von Krauskopf

Why would you consider Appreciative Inquiry in an interview process? Let's start with you cannot create outstanding teams without outstanding people. Far too many companies design a cookie cutter interview process that does not consider the unique aspects of the job in its future state. Nor, considering the team and culture of the desired state you strive to attain.

Technical skills are essential in specific fields but even there if the person hired does not have the soft skills, like emotional intelligence, critical thinking, creativity, and adaptability, then they may not add value to your aspirations to build an effective and efficient team.

Have you ever interacted with someone who is brilliant yet very difficult to converse with or understand? Should they have a role where they are required to teach, guide, explain, collaborate, lead others, or merely interact to ensure productive and efficient work is achieved, then soft skills are essential.

Numerous articles in leading business magazines and reports show the non-technical *"soft skills"* required to excel and be adaptable to a changing global market environment are the least taught and the most needed for interactive success.

We are not talking about some fuzzy and warm attributes that make someone nicer, although that might be a pleasant side effect. Workforces are increasingly diverse and creative in their structure which means engagement and relationship interactions are critically important. An article from the Society for Human Resource Management (SHRM) *"HR's Hard Challenge: When Employees Lack Soft Skills"*[xiv] puts it like this:

> **"Soft skills—which are needed to communicate effectively, problem-solve, collaborate, and organize—are becoming more important for success as the workplace evolves socially and technologically. The rub is that recruiters and employment experts report a "soft skills gap," especially among young workers who are more accustomed to texting than talking, that forces organizations to hire many candidates who fall short on interpersonal abilities."**

While soft skills are slightly more difficult to ascertain it is not complicated to build a measurable process to use for interviewing externally, internally and with succession planning. At DvK Partner Group we design quantifiable outcomes for every On-Boarding program, coaching and team building training we do and include an option for online or in-person follow up sessions that address and enhance employee uptake as the skills develop through use. We do not wish to be a *"one-time"* workshop; we want to build a relationship that aids our clients' ongoing success.

There are also numerous online tools where you can buy both 360 and emotional intelligence assessments to measure performance. If we can measure the necessary soft skills for performance, we can undoubtedly interview for them. If however, we continue with interviewing processes that tick off a box in education and years worked, along with the same old behavioral interview questions that an online search provides the perfect response to then we may miss out on talent that could make a difference.

Add to this the significant cost of recruitment when new hires do not work out or are the wrong fit for a workgroup or customer base. The SHRM Human Capital Benchmarking Survey[xv] in 2017 indicates **the average turnover is at 18%, but interestingly, the average high-performer turnover rate is significantly less, at only 3%.**

There is a real financial benefit to building high-performance teams, which are relationship-based, and yes, that means advanced communication skills and emotional intelligence to build adaptability, resilience, change readiness, critical thinking, to name a few.

While these skills make a positive difference in wellness and interactions, we will keep the focus on the tangible financial impact. Huffington Post regularly shares a Deloitte analysis that indicates turnover cost is tens of thousands of dollars, to the tune of 1.5-2.0x the employee's annual salary. They share other sources, including a paper from the Centre for American Progress that cites **"the average economic cost to a company of turning over *highly skilled jobs* is 213% of the employees' annual salary."** They also provide a formula for you to calculate your organization's costs.

**(Hiring + On-Boarding + Development + Unfilled Time)
x (Number Employees x Annual Turnover Percentage)
= ANNUAL COST OF TURNOVER**[xvi]

We can calculate some startling numbers to make a point here, but I expect you will understand that hiring is a substantial investment. To personalize it, take the last year's vacancies at your organization and use this formula to see the impact. The numbers speak for themselves; you cannot afford to dismiss the potential of soft skills, including the tool of Appreciative Inquiry in building engaged, high-performance teams and for making the right hiring decisions.

Consider these three candidates for a senior leadership role that asks for a minimum bachelor's degree and five years of experience in the job posting. Who would you screen in for an interview?

- **Candidate A:** Has a degree that is 20 years old and does not show any ongoing learning or development on their resume. He has been in the same role for 15 years.

- **Candidate B:** Does not have a degree, has 15+ years of leadership experience that showcases the required expertise, has been promoted 2x and has numerous certificates and courses over the years adding to leadership and skills development relevant to the position.

- **Candidate C:** Has a master's degree not relevant to the role in question, no experience in the area of expertise you are looking for and has five years' experience in two companies.

Who is the best person for the role? There is no "perfect choice" here and all may be great choices. Often recruitment programs short-list from a standardized criteria threshold. Those not meeting a certain number of years, an education standard, a specific skill is screened out. Who have you screened out by limiting with strict parameters and then been unsatisfied with the quality of candidates interviewed?

75% of careers are derailed for reasons related to emotional competencies, including the inability to handle interpersonal problems; unsatisfactory team leadership during difficulty or conflict; or inability to adapt to change or elicit trust.
~Center for Creative Leadership

You cannot hire people that are screened out; you also cannot hire those that don't even apply. If your recruitment process is limiting applicants based on narrow parameters and automated rejections, you may not be in a position to compare three excellent possibilities. What people have amassed in *"skill"* is not the sum of who they are or what they will deliver to your organization.

While the Human Resources industry has had a long-running mantra of *"Hire for Attitude, Train for Skill"*[xvii] it hasn't always been received well by departmental decision makers. It makes sense, and business.com shared a brilliant example of this age-old struggle. The hiring manager wants someone *"who can hit the ground running and has already been able to demonstrate a certain level of skill in the industry or job type they are applying for."*

Unfortunately, as shown above, the real cost of a hiring error is impactful. I have heard many friends in Human Resources say they worked with the manager's expectations and *"hired the best of the lot"* (without much enthusiasm), only to be recruiting for that same role again in a year or two.

Let's explore a different option. As a leader, you want to get the best person for the job. Creating a screening process that encapsulates hard and soft skills will give you a broader and more robust candidate pool. When interviewing, skill set, and experience are of course key considerations when creating parameters to assess and qualify candidates.

However, if you build soft skill requirements that showcase a person's attitude, behavior, and cultural fit you will create stronger teams.

Most organizations have an option to upload a cover letter, as do most recruitment companies. A standard cover letter tends to highlight the attached resume you are going to read already, though I have heard from many managers they don't read them at all. More often than not these become a blurred series of near identical sales pitches from each candidate that replicate a template from online.

Make better use of this attachment option by asking candidates to respond specifically to two questions in their cover letter. Receiving responses to both a behavioral and situational question in the cover letter will provide you with better insight into who they are then what most cover letters offer today. This slight modification to your recruitment process is a straightforward way to incorporate soft skills assessment into your current pre-screening process.

First, a situational question to seek insight into technical skills, which are usually defined through education *or* vocational training. Second, a behavioral problem aimed at assessing transferable or soft skills which are more often attained through combined experiences in life, career, and their initiative in personal development.

Create a question where you ask the candidate to describe how they would specifically react and respond to a scenario you provide them.

The aim is to find out how a candidate would manage a problem that is likely to arise within the workgroup for which they are applying.

This technique is solution based seeking the *"who, what, where, when, why and how"* answers and most effective when they are created to resolve a dilemma. To score soft skills on this type of question, you will assess and measure the way they respond, as appropriate to your question.

The categories you may consider are listed in the next pages. These overarching section examples can be modified to include any unique or role specific aspects to ensure the best person for the job moves forward.

Collaboration / Team Skills:

- *How well did the candidate indicate a team attitude in resolving challenges?*
- *Did they show accountability and ownership of situations?*
- *Were they agile and adaptable to change?*
- *Did they relate shared vision?*
- *Did they stretch themselves beyond basic job tasks?*

Communication / Interpersonal Skills:

- *Did the candidate take ownership, show empathy, and resolve the conflict with a peer or with a difficult client?*
- *Are their responses showing a respectful mannerism?*
- *Did they share information and value a group effort?*

Organizational Skills:

- *How did the candidate respond to team prioritization or integrate department work?*
- *Did they detail how they managed their time well, delegated appropriately, sought assistance to overcome obstacles?*

Decision-making Skills:

- *How did the candidate respond to a strategic action, an ethical situation or manage a diversity scenario?*

- *Did they identify the "vital few" objectives and performance indicators to show they focus on the right things?*

Cultural Skills:

- *How well did the candidate's response align with the culture of your organization now and for the future?*

Emotional Intelligence Skills:

- *How did the candidate respond to situations requiring self-awareness or self-regulation?*
- *Did they seek to understand and show motivation to scenarios requiring a self-starter or empowered mindset?*
- *Did they demonstrate empathy in situations with a fellow employee or customer?*

Leadership Skills:

- *Did they describe their style in a way that aligns with the group culture?*
- *Were they results-driven and did they have a repeatable process to set and achieve goals?*
- *Have they led a team through a crisis or stressful situation well?*
- *Did they show respect towards others, even when detailing mistakes?*
- *Were they able to leverage differing perspectives to build a better end product?*
- *Did they foster innovation and celebrate successes?*
- *Did they champion creative and forward-thinking behavior?*
- *Did they align their accomplishments with the overall corporate strategy and objectives?*
- *Did they empower and develop their team(s) to next level success?*

I have not provided specific questions to ask as each of you will have different job knowledge and particular role aspects that make sense to your industry, department, and culture. It is essential to design questions that are realistic to the environment and the culture the candidate is applying to.

I have developed a portfolio of hundreds of questions to pull from, pending the role; in time you will have that as well. Should you require assistance in this area, I am happy to consult with your organization to build out a more specific guideline for your human resource and management interviewers.

This technique should also be interwoven into your face-to-face interviews and have at least one of those questions be a follow-up to what they submitted in the *"cover"* letter responses. First to ensure they actually wrote and experienced the situation detailed. Second, if you softly challenge their approach to a scenario, *"what else did you consider before choosing this response?"* You can further assess their openness to feedback and adaptability in considering other options.

Your behavioral pre-qualifying question should also link to your organizational culture. What behaviors are vital to the candidate's success? This is commonly used with the STAR interviewing technique (Situation-Task-Action-Result) that helps reveal how a candidate behaved in previous work situations.

This format will help you design scenarios and create a rating or scoring matrix. There are a number of them online should you need help or connect with me for further coaching in this area.

Generally, questions begin with:

- **Tell me about a time ...**
- **Could you give me an example of when...**
- **Walk me through ...**
- **Describe how you would manage ....**

They tend to assess one or more of the following qualities:

- **Teamwork**
- **Problem Solving Attitude**
- **Leadership Skills**
- **Initiative**
- **Interpersonal**
- **Communication Skills**
- **Emotional Intelligence**
- **Cultural Fit**

Since most behavioral interview questions are open-ended and conversational, you need to provide parameters to keep their responses reasonably short.

A more *"open-directed"* questioning approach is more practical and surprisingly not often taught in communication skills programs unless they are related predominately to the psychology or law enforcement fields.

Open-ended questions allow a wide-open response and are instrumental in relationship building. At times, we want to narrow the path to specific responses so you would choose an open-directed question instead.

"Thank you for sharing ABC Project. I would like to know more about how the team worked together when you faced a challenge, and what your specific role was within the team?"

Designing your pre-qualifying questions would follow this route, so you don't get 20-page submissions. Request specific parameters and you get the added bonus of evaluating how well a person pays attention and follows instructions.

A Fire Chief once shared that he designs a precise recruitment process, with step-by-step application rules. Some are not the usual course of application steps that candidates would be familiar with in other job applications. His purpose is to evaluate someone's ability to follow instructions within the exacting parameters provided. It assessed their attention to detail and how coachable they were, undoubtedly fundamental aspects of a stellar Fire Service recruit. I am sure you can agree there is a significant benefit to these essential skills in any organization.The accepted applicants are training in situations where lives are dramatically impacted: the victims, the peer firefighters and the applicant's own life. Being able to follow instructions is a crucial element to a candidate's success.

This can be a useful lesson if the position you are hiring for has specific parameters to follow or an in-depth training process. Every job is different, hence the reason you want to create open-directed questions that best suit the role you are recruiting for, internally and externally.

Using the STAR process is an effective way to ensure you have developed a measurable question that can comparatively assess results during a recruitment process. You can find STAR templates and top behavioral interview questions readily online.

Situation: Frame a specific situation that is relevant to the position they are applying for, i.e., "Tell me a specific challenge you had regarding managing ga diversity or culture situation within your workgroup, and how you handled it?"

Task: What was their role in managing the situation?

Action: What did they do? What were the specific steps taken to manage the situation. What follow up actions and communications, did they prepare?

Results: What was the outcome? What were the lessons learned?

Now that you are all set with the assessment of soft skills let's return to the value of Appreciative Inquiry in an interview process. While we have our process steps outlined well, there is a valuable and important aspect of recruitment to ensure you get the absolute best candidate for the role.

It begins by laying the foundation for a process and environment where you can assess the best the candidate has to offer. Many people associate interviews with fear and anxiety and will immediately break into a sweat, fumble their words, or forget their best examples. If your role requires someone with the capacity to keep their cool under pressure, that may be an evaluation check mark.

However, the vast majority of positions do not have the same intensity of a job interview, so it is up to you to create a safe place, build rapport and interview the best out of the short list you have chosen. The Appreciative Inquiry interview style helps to ease the stress of being evaluated and, as many candidates indicate, a feeling of pressure or fear of being judged.

To evaluate soft skills, you want to replicate the environment they will be working in as best as possible. If it is a team environment, you would want the person to feel comfortable enough to open up and interact with an authentic version of themselves, not a hyper-vigilant interviewee trying to say what they think you want to hear. You are seeking clear insight into their behavior and personality to ensure the best fit for both the culture of your organization and the team they will join.

One of the reasons my company puts a focus on soft skills training as a strategic objective is that positive work cultures and effective change initiatives thrive when employees have these skills. Sadly, they are rarely taught in schools or learned at home with any concerted effort even though they are entirely learnable skills. A vast majority of employees haven't acquired them through life experiences, and this lack of a critical talent holds back the potential of teams and organizations.

The more technical, educated or *"skilled"* the role the less likely the person is to have any expertise in the finer art and science of interaction, rapport, agility, adaptability, critical thinking in a communication arena or with emotional intelligence. Their educational focus remained pinpointed on a narrow band of expertise.

Designing your questions from a situational and behavioral format does not mean they only have to be aimed at adverse scenarios. Adding in a couple of negative examples may be helpful in understanding their fit under stress or within a specific team or organization dynamic where you know such issues may be faced.

However, too much focus on the worst days or situations limits understanding of how the candidate will behave in their day-to-day work as it relates to collaboration, cooperativeness, coachable, agility or rapport building interactions.

Using negative framing alone does not provide you with the insight to measure how they handle innovation, change, team building, customer experience and adaptability as well as positive framing will.

Framing Positive Questions

When we ask questions of an interviewee, what kind of response are we expecting? If we ask questions that can come across as negative or critical, we can expect that kind of answer.

By using positive language, we put the other person at ease; they will feel more confident in their responses and engage more authentically in the interview. It is also a great way to assess their energy and commitment. Balance the process with positive experience questions to help the person share their skills and ambitions. All the while you are determining how they work with the team and the company.

SAMPLE QUESTIONS:

- *"What were the top three things you liked most about your previous role?"*

- *"What do you value most in a team?" "What leadership traits inspire you to do your best work?"*

- *"Tell me about a time where your contribution influenced a significant and positive change to your work environment."*

- *"If you could have changed anything in your previous role, what is it?"*

- *"If you could design a perfect working environment, what would it look like?"*

- *"Tell me about a project, initiative or unique work objective that you were involved with. What was the most satisfying part of the work?"*

- *"Describe the best mentor you've had so far. What traits do you emulate from that experience?"*

- *"Share your best customer interaction with us. What factors made it significant to you?"*

Entice Positive Stories

I have been recruited or "tapped on the shoulder" to interview for nearly every position in my corporate career. When prompted "do I have any questions" either before we begin or at the end of the question period I will ask "what are the top three challenges of this role" and secondly, "from your different perspectives how would you describe the most successful candidate for this role?" I would expect and hope for an explanation aligned with the strategic vision and cultural fit.

The challenges answer would give you great insight on what areas you would need to focus on, and if you had not covered your skillset in those areas in the interview, you could add in a follow-up example.

Surprisingly, in more than one interview the reply would quickly devolve into issues, complaints, problems and how the previous manager failed, quit unexpectedly leaving a mess behind or couldn't handle the workgroup. While there is some benefit to knowing what you are getting into, there were a couple of times I regretted entering the room, I couldn't wait to leave, and those are the roles I declined.

The candidate may be seeking a role; however, this is a good reminder that they are also assessing their interest in working for your organization over the long term. If they do not have a very positive outlook on the organization from the start, do you think they will bring their "A" game to the role? They may still proceed if they *"need"* the job or the raise, but it isn't with enthusiasm beneficial to the company. When you open your interview with positive framing and ask questions that entice rapport and engagement, you are both creating a safe space to evaluate each other effectively.

Positive questioning allows for assessment of their best interactions, experiences and efforts and their personal qualities for cultural fit. The comfort that comes when a person shares their version of a great situation is very telling of their behavioral preferences. Is this candidate a team player, how did they seek collaboration, share in the successes, and feel about contributing to the objective?

Often people know how to respond to behavioral questions quite well. There are hundreds of books and articles to help you prepare for interview questions that ask about *"bad scenario"* questions. Be creative with your scenario questions. Very few interview guidebooks delve into the next layer of insight to assess the soft skills needed in handling specific scenarios. In their answers, you will see the way they interact with others, what they value and how they perceive themselves in a team and within the role. Should they not be a fit it will show clearly enough while maintaining a positive interview.

Probing

Now the focus becomes how to positively challenge and probe a candidate's skills in a way you can authentically assess their cultural fit. Compatibility has to work for both the organization as well as for the prospective employee. Identify the most critical hard skills a candidate requires first, and then focus on the soft skills.

- **Does the work require a specific level of experience?**

- **Which of these skills are transferable or learnable vs mandatory?**

- **How will you assess whether they are a good fit for the present and future culture?**

- **What questions will you prepare to assess Emotional Intelligence?**

- **What questions will you use to assess how adaptable**

- **Will candidates be able to meet future changes?**

- **Do they have the adaptable energy to contribute when future changes occur?**

- **Do they have a positive, empowered outlook?**

Identify the most critical soft skills based on the team dynamic and organizational culture. Ensure those hiring with you understand that a lack of these skills can impact a person's overall wellness.

Consider the maturity of someone's fit with questions that assess the cornerstones of a person's attitudes, ethics, adaptability, emotional management, and communication skills. This insightful awareness of an individual's wellness will be beneficial to the leader and team.

Questions identifying:

- *Social and self-awareness*

- *The perceiving, understanding, and managing of emotions*

- *Their relationship and self-management confidence*

Recurring Themes

When interviewing, recognize the recurring themes that each candidate shares in their answers. Are there patterns in what they have experienced and achieved, and what do those patterns have in common?

They may include transferable expertise, coach-ability, team-player, rapport builder, or signs of arrogance, selfishness, close-mindedness, intolerance etc.

When you recognize the recurring themes, you can evaluate which one, or ones, are the most important and which one you favor the most for the company culture and team they will be joining to maximize fit and fast integration.

Illustration

Debra was interviewing an employee that has been with the company for some years. She could tell he was a little nervous, but she wasn't sure how to make him feel more at ease.

After speaking with him for a while, she asks him what his favorite tasks were in his current role. She noticed how excited he became and how he began to describe a time when he and his colleague worked together and solved a challenging manufacturing problem. Then another time when he was able to resolve a complicated customer issue with one of their products.

She encouraged him to share his stories, noticing how comfortable he was feeling now. She asked him to pull out the positive characteristics of his other tasks, and she began to see a pattern emerge.

Debra noticed he had similar qualities in all of his work and that he had useful skills that would merge well with the team she was hiring for. She also noted the positive interactions and excitement for challenges he displayed. Knowing the projects coming up in her department she knew he would be a good fit for the collaborative nature required for success in this challenging role.

When asked about people he had challenges working with his responses showed a pattern that he did not fit well with negative, uncooperative, and arrogant people. He also said that he liked straightforward and innovative discussions where everyone shared their expertise. It would work well with the Manager's personality and leadership style.

Before he left, she thanked him for sharing his experiences and was glad to see him smiling. It felt good to feel she got a sense of what he might bring to the role.

Debra used that friendly, positive seeking questioning technique for all her interviews after that and was delighted with the results and extremely confident she chose the right person for the job.

Do not let what you cannot do,
Interfere with what you can do!
~John Wood

CHAPTER 8

REALITY CHECK

An intense anticipation itself transforms possibility into reality; our desires being often but precursors of the things which we are capable of performing.
~Samuel Smiles

Anticipatory reality is beneficial in Appreciative Inquiry as it focuses on the future and what we are striving to achieve. Anticipatory reality begins with creating a vision of the future and then determining what can help you get there. Knowing new input will impact the path, we can adapt with ease, change things, add new themes, and make new goals - we are all constantly evolving our anticipatory reality.

Visioning a Successful Future Affects the Present

We are aware that our past does not have to determine our future. However, how we plan our future can affect our present. Thinking ahead to a more prosperous future can increase our positivity today. As I shared earlier, your subconscious is a powerful, flexible, supercomputer that is designed to deliver on the orders we command of it.

Scientifically it is best described as unconscious cognition by neuroscientists and psychologists as the power of the unconscious influence with perception, learning, thought and language in our cognitive thinking process.

Studies, like the one done at the University of Amsterdam, identify *"Accumulating evidence demonstrates that unconscious information processing can influence behavior or trigger cortical activity previously seen as the domain of conscious cognition. Recently unconscious information has been observed to influence even "high-level" cognitive functions, such as task selection, inhibitory control, and decision-making."*[xviii]

All this to say, what we think about and what we say to ourselves matters! We can influence our state of mind with positive intention, knowing that we can achieve that envisioned future and seek the best way to accomplish our goals through our internal and external communications.

Benefits:

- **Positive outlook**
- **Goal successes**
- **Improved focus**
- **Control over current state**
- **Healthier adaptable minds**

Positive thinking also has significant health benefits although the experts have various explanations and reasons why. Insights include better coping skills, improved stress management and overall, the happier you are, the healthier lifestyle you tend to enjoy.

The Mayo Clinic shares that *"researchers continue to explore the effects of positive thinking and optimism on health."*[xix]

Health benefits provided by positive thinking may include:

- **Increased life span**
- **Lower rates of depression**
- **Lower levels of distress**
- **Improved resistance to the common cold**
- **Increased psychological and physical well-being**
- **Better cardiovascular health**
- **Reduced risk of death from cardiovascular disease**
- **Stronger coping skills during hardships and times of stress**
- **Controlling negative anticipation**

Some of us are the type of people who automatically assume the worst in every situation. These individuals start to anticipate anything that can go wrong and try to determine how they would handle what comes up but end up spinning as they are hung up on the negativity. This can also be said to lead to a self-fulfilling prophecy.

You can usually recognize negative anticipation quickly as we all have moments, however, left unchecked it can damage our work and personal relationships. It often shows up with negative self-talk or cognitive distortion where we convince ourselves of something that we have no factual basis to know as truth.

It is essential to identify excessive negativity in the workplace as these are the typical behavior indicators that could lead to a poisoned or toxic work environment if left unchecked. A good leader wants to recognize the warning signs and focus intently on guiding the team towards a more positive path of thinking and interactions. From a wellness perspective, extremes of these traits need more dedicated professional support. Psychology based treatments like, Cognitive Behavior Therapy helps treat variations that can spin into anxiety, depression, and antisocial ways.

While it is good to recognize and expect your team to work towards positivity, you are not a therapist, and this information is for awareness purposes only. If you notice a member of your organization might benefit from expert intervention, then reach out to your Human Resources professional for guidance on how to manage the concern. You may recognize some of the following traits, in various extremes within yourself and others, adapted from Psych Central.[xx]

Narcissistic Viewpoints reflect the "it's all about me" aspect. What others choose, say, or do must have something to do with them. It's when someone having a bad day snaps at a person, and they spin it in their mind determining it was a directed attack on them as they view most situations through a single lens or filter with them as the center of attraction. Removing the positive aspects and only focusing on the negative detail until any good fades from our recall of the situation. This is often the classic

"Eeyore" character of Winnie the Pooh, seeing a glass half empty.

Jumping to Conclusions without considering all the facts or possibilities or expecting a specific adverse outcome without reasonable input. Often showing up in unfounded gossip and rumors or the break down in recounting an event. What we know happens in the "grapevine" effect where the story gets distorted more and more with each retelling.

Black and White, or Polarized thinking whereby we dismiss any grey zone in favor of all or nothing, or either/or perspectives that are hard for anyone else to meet. In leaders you may see this as an inability to delegate, reflecting a view that "no one does this exactly as I do so their work is not up to par," versus understanding there are variations in how to approach and complete "most" tasks to acceptable standards.

Overgeneralizing or painting a new scenario of a remembered event with only a bit of information, spinning into a foregone conclusion that this "thing" will continue to happen again and again. A leader may micromanage everyone because of that one time a member of their team messed up, and they were embarrassed by it.

External Control Fallacy, when we feel no power over outcomes, that some external influence "made us do poorly," basically the classic finger pointing

outward and everywhere but never towards self. When it falls internally one can feel a responsibility for the pain and happiness others feel and believe themselves at fault without confirming any actual direct causation.
An employee who frets about someone's bad mood thinking they are responsible for making it better, to their detriment.

Entitlement or Fairness Fallacy a belief that something is only fair or just when it serves our view of what we consider "fair." When one always judges from a self-serving perspective of what is unfair or fair and grows disenchanted with many things, especially in a workplace. There is substantial commentary relating various extremes of this with the Millennial generation where some say that giving out rewards for mediocre or low efforts has led some to feel an expectation for accolades or benefits that are undeserving or unexceptional.

The Critical Observer who feels everyone "should" conform to a specific standard of acceptance. Externally, this is observed when someone expresses that any variance from "my way is the only right way of thinking or doing" as if someone is breaking the rules. Those that fail to meet this exacting standard build a feeling of frustration, resentment or anger that is known or felt. Internally it can lead to excessive guilt and self-esteem bashing as they beat themselves up over the things, they "should" do better.

This mindset would be typical of a leader in the Military or Emergency Services where exacting rules must be followed. The "I must win, at all costs" mindset is more attached to proving themselves right than considering alternatives, being empathic to how they make others feel in the argument and whose emotions often overtake their logic when things get heated.

Self-Labelling with a global lens instead of a more contextual one. Generalizing a negative branding of a person's or their own entire being rather than focusing on the actual situational aspect. This personality will show with "you always," "you never" statements. Mislabeling specific actions with global labels tends to be emotionally charged and is often seen in personal arguments.

Idealizing Personalities, you are perfect, if you'd only change this…that…oh and one more thing. When a person sees another through a lens of how they would prefer them to be or act, versus their authentic self. That expectation of change, often subconscious at the beginning is required to continue their acceptance and happiness with another and more often than not leads to disappointment in relationships, "I love you, now change."

In the workplace, you may see it when leaders don't "walk their talk." They may ask people to share their ideas, offering open door policies, stating they are ready to coach but then repeatedly tell the other they are wrong and expect everything to be "their better, proven way" instead of being open to new possibilities. This can stagnate innovation, dissolve the trust and leads to high turnover and dysfunctional teams.

Catastrophic Mindset "The Sky is Falling; The Sky is Falling." Those with this thinking will find problems using a "what if" framing that maximizes potential threats and impacts, causing havoc on change initiatives. They will create problems and have their team members chasing down risks and issues that don't exist. This personality creates tension and eventual apathy, like the boy who cries wolf story. When a leader is hyper-focused on latest or potential crisis, the group burn out, and change fatigue is high.

You are learning to understand and identify negative traits but how do you monitor for them? All of the more critical personality traits above can be quickly defined by higher-than-average absenteeism, sick leaves, high turn-over, low morale and toxic teams.

Often both low functioning leadership and teams require nothing more than the tools of advanced communications and emotional intelligence. Remember earlier when I said these skills are not generally learned, but they have such compelling advantages to self and relationships that it transforms mindsets once understood.

As with many things, awareness is a starting point for change. We have seen incredible changes from Executive level to front-line levels with a bonus of wellness through improved home relationships. When the home life is functioning well, people show up to work with a stronger core of wellness and handle their roles and interactions more efficiently and effectively.

When people begin to understand the brain science behind their autopilot responses, a shift in how they view things occurs. When they comprehend, they have the power to shift their emotional auto-response, the benefits in their day-to-day life make it worthwhile to continue self-development towards more positive framing.

An article in Popular Social Science explains it as *"The self-fulfilling prophecy"* is a concept used by the American sociologist Robert Merton to describe how a statement may alter actions and therefore become true. *"In situations where many individuals act from an expectation, they may actually influence whether an incident will take place or not. When this is happening, the individuals create the very conditions they believe exist. Even when there is no reason to worry, the feared outcome may take place if enough people act as if there were some basis for the fear."*[xxi]

That is a powerful concept to grasp and recognizing it and challenging our way of thinking has immediate and hugely beneficial outcomes. Knowing we can learn to stop these negative anticipations, open ourselves up to a broader perspective and consider alternatives is empowering. It doesn't mean you will evaluate in a new way and not still choose a predetermined response, but you are doing so with higher emotional intelligence. Possibility thinking doesn't mean one has to change, only that you are willing to consider alternatives before deciding on an action. That makes it easy to accept and also easy to forgive oneself if you slip into previous ways of thinking during a situation; now you will recognize that you did and can consider why you did and how it impacts your decisions next time.

Our training infuses all this knowledge with a substantial "WIIFM" factor, (what's in it for me). By combining the science and easy practicality in win-win scenarios, we ensure even the most negative people begin to see the benefit of a new way of communicating with others and themselves. Using catch phrases such as *"what's the worst scenario I can live with"*[xxii] and *"what's the added value in this"*[xxiii] provides parameters to embrace this new framing.

This approach is why it's so successful with low employee engagement, low wellness indicators or even toxic environments. It's worth the attempt, and the results are immediate in all areas of their life. It isn't a program where they have to remember to say this when that happens and that when this happens. It's about a proven way of being that dramatically improves relationships and personal wellness.

Once you can prove the benefits of viewing the positive aspects of a situation, employees are less apprehensive about change and feel more confident about their ability to adapt and embrace a new future. Regardless of how big or scary a situation may seem, remaining positive and being a part of the process of change rather than a perceived victim of it can open up possibilities and give the person a strong sense of control over their future.

Being part of the process through Appreciative Inquiry techniques can bring about a sense of ownership and enthusiasm to embrace new horizons. Just being aware of triggers that negatively impact our ego state, as we learned in Chapter 2, helps manage our response.

Examples:

- **Watch for hidden negative thoughts or assumptions; is it fact or emotion?**

- **Avoid jumping to conclusions, ask questions, gather information, and see your place in a new tomorrow.**

- **Recognize the problem is the situation, it's not you.**

- **Decide to understand and influence the change to gain the best possible future.**

- **Influence current situations positively**

The decisions we make today can influence how we see things later. When we limit our negative anticipations and concentrate on creating a positive outlook, our current choices and thoughts begin to develop into an open and proactive manner of thinking. This mindset can improve our overall confidence and internal strength, creativity, and drive to tackle what comes our way.

Unnecessary fretting about the issues and risks is draining and unproductive. When we view these aspects as challenges, we turn that drain into energy to fix and create better outcomes.

- *We can choose to change our thoughts and question automatic negativity through fact-finding exercises.*

- *We can decide to open up to opportunities and ideas that can influence our planning.*

- *We can evolve our decision-making process by positive influence that stretches us to seek innovative and "next practice" answers.*

- *We can grow our adaptability and critical thinking skills to prepare for a global environment that will influence constant change.*

Benefits:

- **More confidence in your decisions**
- **Less negative or anxious feelings**
- **Positive outlook on future decisions**

Without fear, why try? Without hope, why change?
~ James MacNeil

Critical Thinking uses Data and Real Examples

One of the unproductive aspects of negative anticipatory reality is that we often base our thoughts and conclusions on things that we have overplayed in our heads. Some of us go beyond the classic over thinking to "the sky is falling," catastrophic thinking, defined as *"ruminating about irrational worst-case outcomes,"* by a *Psychology Today* article[xxiv] *which confirms "you must first identify it for what it is, an irrational worst-case scenario. The second step, identify best-case scenarios."*

If one begins to think about the worst thing that could happen or that it could all blow up in their face but has nothing to base it on, then they are hurting themselves unnecessarily. The best outcomes are detailed with a healthy risk and reward balance. Instead, acknowledge concerns and risks, but then focus on the facts of a problem to identify what needs to have a contingency designed for it.

If this seems challenging, then reframe each of your particular concerns with the question "what's the worst-case scenario I am willing or able to live with" and "what's the most favorable outcome I can hope for?" Now you have a more defined risk to tackle and will be considering it from a logical framework.

As example:

You begin to feel stressed because you forgot to turn in a monthly report to your manager. You can feel the panic rising and start thinking of the worst-case negative possibilities that could come from this situation, from being reprimanded up to getting fired.

STOP, list out and review the facts and data that are pertinent and begin to assemble a more balanced approach by assessing both negatives and positives. If you know that your work is consistently on time and that the manager is reasonable, they will most likely understand with a rational explanation. Perhaps you will recall that he/she has told you before that if something comes up, just let them know.

Once you've reviewed the facts of the situation versus the fatal doomsday scenario you have created in your mind, you will feel less worried about the oversight and feel more confident about correcting your initial panic, moving forward with a more objective mindset.

This reaction is often true of "stories" you hear as well; when you read that outlandish post on social media or the email from a co-worker, STOP, and ask, is it factually accurate or has the story grown out of proportion or even correct at all? A little fact checking on the rackets or accounts that our mind creates or accepts will save us all a lot of grief and stress.

Avoid Immediate Firm Conclusions Regarding

- "Word of Mouth" stories

- **The "maybe" or "what if" scenarios that spin negatively in your mind.**

- **Dramatized outcomes or over-reaction**

- **Jumping to conclusions without assessing all possibilities**

- **Outlandish or harmful stories that are unverified through a legitimate source**

Before you speak ask yourself if what you are going to say is true, is kind, is necessary, is helpful.
If the answer is no, maybe what you are about to say should be left unsaid.

~ Bernard Meltzer

Practical Illustration

Bruce was finishing his report on the new accounting software and preparing to show it to his manager. He wanted to believe his manager would like it and would credit him and the work of the team, but he wasn't confident how it would go over with him. He began to doubt himself and doubt if the software was fit for the company.

He became obsessively worried that the manager would overlook his numbers and make decisions that didn't benefit anyone. That maybe it would hurt his upcoming performance review and he really needed that raise and... Bruce finally caught himself, remembering his High-Performance Team Building training and the Stop, Drop and Roll concept.

He told himself to "STOP," realizing he was overreacting, "DROP" the fatalistic thinking without any concrete evidence and "ROLL" with what he knew as facts. That he needed to show the report first, trust in his work and accept the feedback before concluding there was even a problem. He told himself to review a more balanced approach, and prepared responses to any issues he felt might be challenged or questioned.

More confident and ready he sat back and waited for his manager's response. When his manager complimented the report findings and the use of the software, Bruce knew he had over thought his reaction too much.

You are what you think.
So just think big,
believe big,
act big,
work big,
give big,
forgive big,
laugh big,
love big and
live big.
~Andrew Carnegie

CHAPTER 9

THE VISIONARY LEADER

*Good business leaders create a vision,
articulate the vision, passionately own the vision,
and relentlessly drive it to completion.*
~Jack Welch

All positive change begins with you. If you are to lead, inspire, and serve your team and organization well, then you need to *"walk the talk"* and present your desired state in your communications, actions, and vision. With this, your team know what they are working to achieve, and it becomes much easier to appreciate their efforts when you are all moving in the same direction.

Now some of you may think that visioning only takes place at the executive level. I suggest when you deliver and discuss the organizational vision with your team, do so until there is a shared understanding of the corporate, department or your workgroup's contribution. Your staff can read a vision or mission statement, but together you provide clarity for aligned commitment and achievement to make it happen.

Consider *"Top in the field,"* folks like Olympians, major sports stars and CEOs who use visualization. We can agree they all may have common goals or statements, a clear objective of winning or success.

It is the internal and expressed dialogue each uses that sets them apart from their competition. How they plan their approaches and set benchmarks to work towards those goal(s) will make the difference competitively.

Groups, teams, and associations may also have a common goal towards success, in this case, they will have to unite their process of obtaining the outcome with others. If they are fractured in thought, they will be working in different directions.

When you do this exercise with your team, and you all walk away with a standard definition of success in working towards your unit or department goals you will discover fantastic productivity comes from this unity and common objective. Visualization is often associated with peak performance, and if creating a more productive, happier team is a goal, then this united mindset exercise is a valuable tool.

Most of us have experienced *"flow"* described in an athletic insight journal as *"an optimal mental state (Csikszentmihalyi, 1990), flow is associated with optimal performance, as well as providing an optimal human experience. Given the psychological skills that are likely to influence flow, it is suggested that imagery may be useful for facilitating flow experiences."*[xxv]

Why would this help in the workplace? Consider a day or an hour that flew by productively, a conversation with a peer that seemed to happen in a blink of an eye and resulted in excellent outcomes. Remember an issue with another department that you had the perfect answer for and with a quick phone call and discussion, it was resolved. These are flow scenarios that happened with we are "on point" with what we want and have the mindset and rapport to make it happen.

I first learned this from a coach who introduced me to the teachings of Lanny Bassham[xxvi] when I was a competitive shooter in the 1980's. Lanny was a Silver Medalist in the 1972 Munich Olympic Games and frustrated with his mental failure during the competition; he sought out training in mental mastery. Unable to find what he needed; he began interviewing Olympic Gold Medalists to learn what they did differently to win. His system, called *"Mental Management,"*[xxvii] is brilliant.

I bought this resource as soon as it became available, and I have highly recommended it for years. It has since expanded to include programs for many sports, teachers, parents, and coaches (find it here: affiliate link, https://is.gd/mentalmgt).

Personally, I have used the techniques for years, as well as in compacity as leader, mentor, or coach when helping others achieve the best version of themselves. The teachings take you through principles, goal setting and affirmations to develop the best version of you in whatever you wish to accomplish.

The overarching takeaways were:

- **Conscious thoughts and mental pictures control our senses; what you think about creates your reality.**

- **The subconscious creates the performance from input repetition.**

- **Your self-image and your performance are aligned, they are the total of your habits and attitudes.**

How does this help you move a visualized goal of a more productive, happier workforce into a reality? By coaching and mentoring the brain science, your team understands they have more control over their thoughts and successes then they may have believed.

Both the conscious and unconscious work with the same things: memory, habits, feelings, behaviors, and emotions. The magic is understanding that the unconscious is the source from which the conscious pulls from, it is the accumulation of what it has been fed by the inputs received.

When you erase something on your computer, the file is still there, hidden. As you install new data, it slowly overwrites the memory space to delete the old programming permanently. The same concept applies when reprogramming your subconscious to pull new and updated information into your conscious mind.

Will you change overnight? Not likely; but a steady feed or input of positive framing, objective and focused visualization will slowly overwrite the years of old, outdated, negative and biased data over time. You are reprogramming through conscious choice and questioning outputs that don't add value to your success and happiness in life. When you do this with your teams, you attain more positive, agile, change accepting staff.

Teaching this process to your teams helps build an understanding that there is something in it for them, in all aspects of their lives. Including visualization in planning sessions with those who report to you, or are mentored by you, helps everyone involved gain aligned clarity about objectives. Good things happen when your team is all working towards a shared vision and understand how their efforts will impact the broader organizational strategic goals.

Which now leads us to the neuroscience of how your brain works. A report named, "The Neural Basis of the Dynamic Unconscious by Heather Berlin states; *"recent imaging, psychophysical, and neuropsychological findings suggest that unconscious processes take place hundreds of milliseconds before conscious awareness."* [xxviii]

What does that mean with relation to brain hacking by visualization? That we are basing our conscious decisions on stimuli usually beyond our cognitive control and that process is fed through our thoughts, beliefs, experiences, biases, and learnings.

When we are actively feeding our subconscious through our conscious decision to upload newly visualized expectations, then it will start finding solutions to give back. It will begin providing ideas to create the desired outcomes from our refreshed "memory and experience vault," individually and in team brainstorming sessions. Positive imagery is a powerful tool in helping us to remain focused on the outcomes we wish to attain and have a more balanced and practical perspective from which to view any challenge or problem.

Even consider it when working to mitigate risks. Risk Management often congers up expectations of adverse outcomes. However, that is not always the case. A thorough risk review will allow the opportunity to consider all the potentials, and it also allows you the ability to plan mitigation strategies. Being prepared and ready for change and iterations in our plans and operations are the positive outcome of a thorough risk review. That is the critical thinking, agile responsive, change ambassador we all wish for in a team member.

Visualizing all the possibilities and the best potential outcomes allows us to embrace the fact that change may bring about bumps in the road. By expecting and preparing for them, they aren't so impactful or stressful.

Leadership is the capacity to translate vision into reality.
~Warren Bennis

Shaping Performance with Positive Imagery

The outcomes of Positive Imagery can often serve as a reminder of good work, but it can also help in a rewarding aspect. As you start seeing an increase in performance and productivity, you can track and measure little successes to build enthusiasm and appreciation for the results. Some physical forms of positive imagery include a competitive game or celebration for meeting measured objectives in the workplace. It could be a trophy or an achievement chart of whatever you measure as an indication of hitting targets. It can even be goofy and certainly doesn't need to cost much.

When leading teams at FedEx we had the rubber chicken award; this comic chicken roused good-natured competition between area teams to meet their goals, and the presentation was fun and uplifting to everyone. Another time, I built a horse race with Velcro pieces on a bulletin board and teams would move their horses as they progressed towards an objective each day over a week. At times it was *"team against team,"* or it would just be meeting a target that needed attention

We made it entertaining at the end of each week with incentives and fun challenges to improve the following week and of course, congratulatory prizes that were promised from previous weeks. It didn't cost much; at times it was home baked muffins the next shift or their manager spent a defined amount of time helping load or offload each driver's truck with them. Our incentives were always framed to help build relationships as well as offer a *"win."*

Performance can be influenced based on the kind of outcome we want to work for, and teams can be energized and motivated by positive imagery. They see and get involved in both their own and the team's progress as they work towards a goal. It promotes collaboration, innovation, and positive discussions about how to improve as well.

Sadly, many workgroups are unaware of the strategic objectives their daily efforts are striving to achieve. Show them tangible progress, and it creates a regular reminder of how well they are doing and allows you, as the leader, to celebrate their efforts and successes in a fun way.

Many small business owners and entrepreneurs use vision boards to set their objectives, and if you felt it would unite your team, you could design one for your workgroup. By making it exciting and engaging you allow people to build positive imagery of their contributions and group dynamics will snowball. Make sure you celebrate wins along the way!

> *Where this is no vision,*
> *there is no hope.*
> *~George Washington Carver*

Be Better Prepared for Adversity

As mentioned before, a healthy Risk Management perspective can be positive. It does not mean you are oblivious to challenges and the things that can go wrong. You can be prepared for the worst, using contingencies and opportunities, *"if X happens, how do we best deal with it?"*

This comfort with risks and challenges dramatically eases the stress when things fail to go entirely to plan. Your preparedness takes the panic out of the moment.

Should you not have a contingency in place for a particular event even the exercise of reviewing other risks removes some of the fear of an unknown. You have prepared your team to consider and discuss potential problems before, with a mindset of how to overcome them.

Being prepared for adversity means that you do not lie to yourself about what can happen. Be cognitive of the situation for what it is. Expect that it can be difficult and may change, but you don't let it damper your focus on the goals and objectives. Being more prepared and open to learning new ways of managing situations allows calmer understanding.

You may not be able to avoid or alter problems that arise in change situations, but you can change your reaction and perspective to any challenges you face.

One of the critical concepts we teach, and coach, is that one has to learn to control oneself first. Then have improved understanding of how to manage interactions before earning the right to influence others, ethically. It must begin with how "**You Manage You**."

Understanding this concept is the foundational aspect of acquiring strong emotional intelligence and advanced communication skills. When taught well and then integrated into the culture, your teams are much more cohesive and adaptive to change because they understand how critical their reactions and actions are with assisting better outcomes for themselves and all involved.

> *We're living in a different world now in terms of employee needs, and companies have to offer alternative methods for getting the work done. Even under the most difficult circumstances, you can have creative flexibility.*
> *~ Anne M. Mulcahy, former CEO Xerox*

The Power of being Flexible and Creative

When a problem presents before you, it may not be feasible to change what has happened or the effect of the problem on anyone else. However, as we teach in our Team Building workshop, you do have control over one thing: yourself, and you can adjust how you view or react to a situation. Through this *"controllable"* aspect you are better able to adapt, accept and have ideas on how to make the best of any situation.

The first step is realizing that with a learned conscious effort you can take the negative connotation away from being faced *"with a problem"* and tap into your creative ability to adapt and overcome obstacles placed in your way.

We are more creative when we look at a problem as having a grey area, or even a prism of possibility rather than thinking there is only one black and white solution. Choosing to focus on what we can control will develop our resiliency.

To do this well, requires us to recognize that we have automatic triggers and reactions based on our personal experiences, knowledge, culture and even our subconscious bias. Accepting this allows us to ponder, intellectually, that perhaps we need more information before concluding that we may not know all the factors when we respond to situations, we consider problematic, often in an emotionalized way.

With practice, you can induce a STOP response internally to halt the automatic emotional reaction to situations we believe to be problematic and consider other possible options for the scenario before deciding how to react. This will develop your ability to be more deliberate and considerate in your responses.

Let's consider a workgroup change is announced and your team, having been trained well on soft skills, is ready to receive this new information. They will now discuss all the positive or interesting aspects that may come from a new work process for instance. How it may free them to do something more meaningful for the end user or teach them a new transferable skill that could help their future career.

Wouldn't this response be more beneficial than spiraling negatively that it automatically means the end of someone's *"currently defined"* job versus the beginning of a new type of job? You would choose a more sensitive approach to helping those who may, in fact, be losing their roles in the company permanently.

If layoffs are inevitable, the approach to accepting change is more aligned to how can each person gain the most advantageous package, workforce training and references to prepare them for their future.

There are skills training needed for any position change, and over time every position evolves. If this is understood well by your teams then altering how we deliver products and services in an ever-modernizing world becomes an expectation as otherwise many jobs will just become redundant. That doesn't mean a loss of work; it means different work. The more your team gets trained in transferable skills and develops adaptability with this continual learning the more they anticipate future growth.

In a globally driven or technologically advancing environment the requirement for innovation, fluidity and adaptability is critical. A term has been coined by the World Economic Forum, the *"re-skilling revolution."*[xxix]

The onus is on corporations to enhance an environment of continuous learning to ensure their workforce stays up to date and ready to transfer into the future roles needed for competitive and service success. "Between now and 2020, the World Economic Forum anticipates growth in demand for:

- **cognitive abilities (52%),**
- **social skills (37%), and**
- **complex problem-solving skills (40%)."**[xxx]

With this global insight, we can expect many organizations will need to seek out and groom individuals with soft skills, agility, change adaptability and critical thinking strengths. Hence the focus in our core training, to blend these necessary foundational skills with the area of focus unique to every client.

We provide a broad range of training including leadership, team building, diversity and inclusion, sales, and project leadership. workshops, training, and coaching, are all uniquely designed, and they each have a cornerstone of Emotional Intelligence and foundational soft skills woven into the curriculum. That is the difference between good skills training and building measurable outcomes for excellence in your people.

Many organizations are planning for continuous change with robust strategies in advancing transferable skills that allow their internal workforce to adapt seamlessly to the evolving jobs of tomorrow. The push towards online courses and gamification learning does not aid this particular type of learning as understanding tends to require an interactive approach or ideally, a blended version of training.

I suggest any interactive based skills are done in person. The role-playing and scenario discussions make this learning stick more than online, which is better for straight skills training. Having this blend of interactive facilitation and online skills building is currently the best approach to modernizing learning while still gaining the core understanding that becomes ingrained through more personal means.

The future of gamification in training may create improved online apps for the interactive aspects. We are exploring this and other technology now, and it looks very promising. I expect the in-person element will still hold the highest return on investment until the next generational changeover. Many baby boomers and GenXer's have yet to embrace the online environment to a level of enjoying app based or gamification learning.

To improve the Change Culture, I also like to infuse the change ambassador concept into all training. In my experience, it has proven that people develop a positive attitude and creative mindset when they are an active member of a change scenario. It empowers people to feel some control over the changes happening and visualize the best possible future state. It also opens up the possibility that by participating you have more likelihood to have some influence in the process and feel more valued and validated for the expertise you can provide.

Remember:

- **You can change even if the problem isn't going to.**
- **You can only control how "you" react.**
- **There are more ways than one way to get results.**
- **The less emotion you attach to a failure or change event, the easier it is to think clearly about solutions.**

"The highest calling of leadership is to unlock the potential of others."
~ Carly Fiorina,
Former CEO, Hewlitt Packard

Practical Illustration

Anna was working on a design project for the new library that was opening soon. After hours of tedious work, she felt as though she wouldn't finish on time or have enough energy to make a great design. Anna began to feel discouraged and depressed.

When she walked back into her office, she saw the small plaque she received after her last design project. It made her smile to remember that she had done something so successful.

She remembered the problems she had on the last project and visualized about how she dealt with them. Anna knew this project was different and had more complexities to it than the last one, but she knew how to use the process and mitigation tools; she had learned to handle issues when they came up.

When she thought of her finished design, she visualized how great the library would look and how it would benefit so many people.

Anna adapted her self-talk to identify the benefits and opportunities which turned her apprehension into excitement. She started a step-by-step process towards a perfect completion. Prioritizing what needed to be done to achieve it and then quickly identifying the potential problems that needed to be mitigated.

She plotted the potential risks and setbacks she might face and contingencies she would use, should a problem arise. She set up brainstorming sessions with all involved and impacted stakeholders and solicited input. She made a list of whom she may need on her team for the different phases and sought resources support.

She confirmed supports to step in and assist should specific events occur.

Feeling more in control, confident and positive, Anna set back to work on her draft Project Plan and move towards Initiation. With her mind freed of pitfalls, she was able to tap into her best creative and impactful possibilities.

1/ Learn how to anticipate the future
2/ Focus on the positive
3/ Fail forward
4/ Obstacles are opportunities in disguise
5/ Take Risks

~Steve Jobs

CHAPTER 10

INFLUENCING WITH EMOTIONAL INTELLIGENCE

You can't order people to do what you want; you must persuade or inspire them to put forth their best efforts toward the clear objective you have defined. Influence competence draws on empathy; without understanding the other person's perspective and sensing their feelings, influencing them becomes more difficult.
~ Daniel Goleman, Author of Primal Leadership

Being influential is similar to casting a stone in a pond, the ripples can have far-reaching effects. Before earning the right to persuade another ethically and to positive ends, we should ensure we have mastered ourselves. Through Appreciative Inquiry, we gain the respect and power to influence through leading by example and assisting others to develop the best version of themselves positively and productively.

Using Strengths to Solve Challenges

Leaders who focus on building the individual strengths within themselves and those they coach will lead high-performance teams. This commitment to focus on employee engagement moves beyond the annual surveys and makes your team dynamic, agile, and customer centric. When employees feel they are valued and have a clear understanding of what they are working to achieve, you have a critical thinking and problem-solving powerhouse that is highly adaptable and solves challenges head-on.

A Gallup poll survey on employee engagement shows proof of this. *"When you see or hear the term "employee engagement," your mind might go straight to your HR department's annual survey. However, that's not how your employees experience engagement. They are engaged -- or disengaged -- every day, not just once a year when they take a survey."*

To your team, engagement is a feeling of wanting to come to work in an environment where they feel like part of something meaningful. Engaged employees go above and beyond expectations. Top-down corporate policies don't give employees that kind of motivation. You do. Every day, you embody the organization's values and culture to your employees. As the manager, you set the tone.

"Almost seven in 10 employees (67%) who strongly agree that their manager focuses on their strengths are engaged. Moreover, when employees strongly disagree with this statement, the percentage of employees who are engaged plummets to 2%."[xxxi]

What result would you prefer? The key is to find what your strengths are and use them to your advantage in developing the individual and collective strengths of your team. Appreciative Inquiry can be used as a self-assessment tool; ask yourself what kind of strengths have worked best for you before.

Ask yourself how you felt when they aided problem resolution. Recall how confident you felt afterwards. Learn the lesson of being kind to yourself and promoting your abilities; it will then quickly transfer to offering the same grace and coaching to others. This exercise should be a standard part of your performance meeting where you are setting employee and team goals and objectives.

Now recall when you struggled to learn something, a time when you relied on another to teach you as you moved towards achieving mastery in an area. Top CEOs and those in succession planning for that level almost always have a coach. Coach-ability at all levels of excellence, whether business, sports, entertainment, or the arts, is recognized as essential for success. The lesson here is obvious, to achieve success we should seek mentoring and coaching to grow our skills.

The best way to build and remember an ability is to teach it to another. Ingrain the process of continual learning into your teams by sharing your development journey. I had always found that sharing my strengths and my weaknesses, asking for and reviewing their 360 feedback, even when there wasn't a formal corporate program, to be very educational and uniting. When you show you are open to learning from your team, they are much more open to learning from you.

If there is a disconnect between what they wish for in their manager and an area of weakness for me, then the team will be a little more understanding and forgiving if I am not meeting their expectations, if say, attempting to do so would lead me to be inauthentic.

It is also powerful to outline as a way to demonstrate that you cannot be all things to all people. Often their wishes are personality based and if everyone is looking for different things you can gently and humorously say you are only one person and not able to develop multiple characters to meet everyone's asks. However, with their guidance and understanding, you will work towards being a consistent leader with empathy that will respect how they wish to be treated within a fair and consistent framework. This simple approach begins their growth in understanding their own personality variations and *Ego States* and how they might be impacting the team dynamic.

Asking the team and seeking their support as I work to improve an area that could be further developed produced fantastic team synergy. You are leading adults; they all have experienced guiding and coaching others in their life so tap into their strengths to create the best version of you while doing the same for them.

I have been told I have a gift of seeing the best version of someone which I believe it comes from actively looking for strengths and potential. I seek what I like about someone when I interact with them and, admittedly, there are times when the best I can come up with is the color of their outfit. This isn't about creating false feelings or being untrue to yourself or others. It's about being curious about others, empathetic to their story, seeking out their strengths and being respectful and interested as you get to know them.

When you build this acceptance and understanding with your team, it changes perspectives on what might have been perceived problematic previously. You are showing that you and they are imperfect and will need to work together to build a cohesive relationship, trusting and relying on each other's value to achieve success together. Dissolving as many barriers as possible to improve interpersonal dynamics allows for more significant innovative and agile mindsets when it comes to operational problems.

This critical thinking skill will also ease coping issues with change as open-mindedness lessens fear, anger, and confusion-based responses that trigger unhelpful emotional reactions. All this leads to improved trust.

Why is trust important in leader and employee relationships? Consider that you may not care if you "like" the person you report to but most of us want to be led by someone trustworthy.

I will share a Washington Post interview question given to the author, Stephen M. R. Covey on his book Speed of Trust, an excellent read that I highly recommend.

> **"Question: What are the most critical components to developing trust?**
>
> **Answer: Credibility and behavior.**
> *Credibility flows from having both character and competence. Our character is who we are; our competence is what we can do.*

"If we're strong in one area and weak in the other, we won't sustain trust in the long run. I might trust an individual with high character but low competence if I went on vacation and needed someone to watch my home because they're honest.

However, I may not trust them on a critical project if they don't have a track record of performing. The reverse is true as well. Someone could be high in competence but low in character. They might get things done, but in doing so, they might also violate the beliefs and values of the agency. That lack of character will undermine trust and credibility."[xxxii]

Too often, people focus only on delivering results, but how we get there will determine whether we sustain trust. Also, if you want to be trusted, you'll need to extend trust, because trust is reciprocal.

One reason why, in many agencies and organizations today, employees don't trust their management is simply that the management doesn't trust the employees, and the employees reciprocate that distrust. Leaders ought to take the first step to extend trust to their employees.

If you create an environment where people's strengths are acknowledged, you work towards mutual trust; if you seek ways to improve the Emotional Intelligence of each individual, then you are on your way to a high-performance team.

How do you relate workplace strengths to Emotional Intelligence? The following chart is adapted from Daniel Goleman's work shows where Emotional Intelligence in the workplace aligns to all shared in this book thus far.

	Self (Personal Competence) Self-Awareness	Other (Social Competence) Social Awareness
Recognition	Emotional self-awareness Accurate self-assessment Self – Confidence Critical Thinking Coachable	Empathy Organizational Awareness Service to Others Body Language Awareness Social Cue Awareness
	Self-Management	Relationship Management
Regulation	Emotional Self-Control Transparency Adaptability Achievement Focus Initiative	Influence Developing Others Change Catalyst Conflict Management Rapport Strength

The importance of Empathy for Social Awareness:

> *"You never really understand a person*
> *until you consider things*
> *from his point of view...*
> *until you climb inside of his skin and*
> *walk around in it."*
> ~Atticus Finch in To Kill A Mockingbird

Empathy is necessary to enable us to have functional societies. There are very few workplace environments where one isn't exposed to other humans and expected to get along. We must, therefore, have some internal insight that enables us to work together regardless of differences, to manage disagreements, and, to communicate productively with each other.

Lack of empathy drives manipulative power, creates toxic divides, and brings out the very worst of us in communications. Devaluing others as insignificant is not a sign of a healthy organization.

Daniel Goleman, author of Focus: Techniques for Excellence describes three levels of Empathy and why they are essential to an Emotionally Intelligent leader.[xxxiii] He writes about a CEO he interviewed who said: *"I like to understand how people see the world. It's always different for each person. I'm fascinated by the ways people think about things, what's important to them, how they put their world together."*

Goleman follows with, ***"That natural curiosity about other people's reality, technically speaking, signifies "cognitive empathy," the ability to see the world through others' eyes... it does more than give us an understanding of their view, it tells us how best to communicate with that person: what matters most to them, their models of the world, and even what words to use or avoid when talking with them."***

Managers with great cognitive empathy, for instance, get improved performance from their direct reports. Also, executives who have this mental asset do well when assigned to a culture different from their own; they can pick up the norms and ground rules of another culture more quickly. However, emotional empathy, a second variety, has different benefits. This empathy depends on a different muscle of attention: tuning in to another person's feelings requires we pick up their facial, vocal, and a stream of other nonverbal signs of how they feel instant-to-instant. This variety of empathy, research shows, depends on our tuning into our own body's emotional signals, which automatically mirror the other person's feelings.

We see the third variety, empathic concern, whenever someone expresses caring about another person. When a leader lets people know that he will support them. It earns trust. Empathy is often confused with pity, sympathy, or compassion, what's the difference?

Pity acknowledges that someone else's suffering exists. It requires very little in the way of emotional involvement, or engagement with the situation you observe. You may see a homeless person as you drive by and pity them but not be compelled to stop and give them money or join a local charity to serve those in that situation.

Sympathy means you care about the suffering of another person. It has a compelling action that often results in expressions of heartfelt exchange on the matter; this is a relatively natural response that leaves you unhappy to hear about someone else's unhappiness. We commonly feel this way when someone we know personally is experiencing a loss in their family. We feel truly sad for them although there may be nothing we can do.

Empathy evokes deeper engagement as you consciously place yourself "in their shoes" and make an effort to understand from their perspective.
You do not necessarily agree with that view or perspective, you may not condone their action or choice, but you have taken the time to understand their stance. This instinctive emotion is very human and quite powerful. It allows those of us with opposing views, cultures, and personalities to be civil and engage together acceptably and productively.

Compassion elevates empathy to a level of taking on the other's feeling with a sense of responsibility and desire to alleviate the suffering. While empathy allows a shared understanding without ownership, compassion elevates the shared experience to a more global and internalized perspective. This feeling motivates many in the social services and caregiving fields and can instigate advocacy and altruism. It also creates a burden on some who take on too much of another's experience or feelings which can lead to compassion fatigue or mental health stresses.

A model designed by Robert Shelton [xxxiv], a psychologist in a Californian high school, is a fantastic snapshot of the differences. Engagement increases as you move from pity to compassion.

Pity: I acknowledge you are suffering.
Sympathy: I care about your suffering.
Empathy: I can feel your suffering.
Compassion: I want to relieve your suffering.

Empathy within a team

Using empathy while listening to another person speak, and while suspending judgement, allows you to honestly, openly, and respectfully *"hear"* the other perspective. As before, I am not advocating that you would agree with the other person only that they have been given the respectful empathy to hear their point of view; this is useful for any productive listening objective.

Empathetic listening helps promote active listening as it opens the listener to consider where the speaker is coming from emotionally, reading the body language and hearing content of his or her words. This skill lets the listener assess what the speaker says and how it is presented more accurately, which ultimately leads to better understanding.

Tips for Being an Open-Minded Listener

- Lose the Ego! Prepare your mind to be open to the information without a preemptive conclusion.

- Make notes. Jotting down items to discuss after someone finishes speaking stops your brain from spinning and seeking a reply before you have heard someone out.

- Remember there is more than one way to do most things. Your approach may be right; someone else's may be just as good. Be open to coaching the best out of someone, not dictating to duplicates of yourself and your way of thinking.

- Establish the areas where you and the other person agree; using notes helps you to focus on this as well.

- Repeat back a summary of the main points you heard to ensure you understand and to confirm for them that they have been heard as they intended.

- Thank them for sharing their insight/input/presentation. Show respect for their communication effort

Satya Nadella, CEO of Microsoft, and author of *Hit Refresh,* stated in an interview with the Washington Post.[xxxv] *"Teamwork was being replaced by internal politics. We were falling behind. While I admired every member of our team, I felt that we needed to deepen our understanding of one another—to delve into what really makes each of us tick—and to connect our personal philosophies to our jobs." He describes leading his team through exercises where they got to know each other a little bit — not as fellow cubicle drones, but as people. You might think of empathy as a motivation that makes you donate, or volunteer, or do some other good deed. Nadella argues that it does far more than that: It opens your mind up to think more about other people's perspectives. "The business we are in is to meet the unmet, unarticulated needs of customers," Nadella says in a recent Wall Street Journal interview. "And there's no way you're going to do that well without having empathy and curiosity."*

Employees who believe that management is concerned about them as a whole person - not just an employee - are more productive, more satisfied, more fulfilled. Satisfied employees mean satisfied customers, which leads to profitability.

~ Anne M. Mulcahy

CHAPTER 11

THE "ME" FACTOR

There is overwhelming evidence that the higher the level of self-esteem, the more likely one will be to treat others with respect, kindness, and generosity.
~ Nathaniel Branden

Building Self-Confidence Will Promote Positive Change

All of our training programs at DvK Partner Group, even the more technical Project Management and Agile training, has essential Emotional Intelligence (EI) teachings weaved into them. It does not matter what you do if you think about it, there are likely people involved so, therefore, mastering your EI is imperative to achieving the pinnacle of success.

Start with yourself! The perception you have of yourself not only affects how other people see you, but it also impacts how they treat you and interact with you. Interestingly, it can also change how you view yourself in the world, act within it and how you treat others.

Emotional Intelligence is described in four quadrants; the first two are the recognition and regulation of personal competence, our self-awareness and self-management, how *"you control you."*

When we put focus and energy outside of ourselves, we lose power in making a significant impact because our focus is on something we most often, cannot control. What we can control, 100%, is how we perceive the situations we face and manage ourselves in reaction and actions. The first two areas of focus are self-development and a significant portion of the 2-days of team building training we do. They relate to work in the following ways:

Self-Awareness

- **Emotional self-awareness**
- **Accurate self-assessment**
- **Self Confidence**
- **Critical Thinking**
- **Being Coachable**

Self-Management

- **Emotional Self-Control**
- **Transparency / Authenticity**
- **Adaptability**
- **Achievement Focus**
- **Initiative**
- **Optimism**

Once we understand the power of controlling ourselves, we can move forward in life with less stress and anxiety about the areas that we cannot control. The next two quadrants of Emotional Intelligence are outward facing.

They include, recognition and regulation of our social competence, and that of our social-awareness and relationship-management. Both are easily learnable and have dramatic influence over your success. They include:

Social Awareness

- **Empathy**
- **Organizational Awareness**
- **Service to Others**
- **Body Language Awareness**
- **Social Cue Awareness**

Relationship Management

- **Influence**
- **Developing Others**
- **Change Catalyst**
- **Conflict Management**
- **Rapport Strength**
- **Teamwork**
- **Collaboration**

Workplace discord often comes from this as many people are very unaware of how their manner and actions impact others. At times low Emotional Intelligence can lead to people not caring what others think, or so they let on. Usually, deep down they care very much, but they do not have the knowledge or tools to better themselves.

Of all of these traits, personally developing self-confidence is the most critical because without it some may struggle to embrace the rest. Providing yourself and your teams with empowering exercises and training to boost this trait can be very beneficial to all. When we learn to remember our earlier successes or imagine a goal we want to achieve with no obstacles, we get an instant confidence boost and can feel better about the choices we make.

When we are focused on wellness in the areas of EI and have healthy self-confidence, self-mastery, social awareness, and relationship management skills, we are more apt to make positive changes without being fearful. We manage better without our internal criticism limiting our potential. Appreciative Inquiry allows the leader to help this self-development journey occur much faster.

Tips to build Self-Confidence at work:

- Present yourself how you want to be perceived, visualize the presence, and create the dress and deportment required to achieve it. Physiologically, these actions will influence your inner thoughts.

- We all have our own bias and cultural influences. Be open to learning about people and areas you do not know. You do not need to consider changing your beliefs or perceptions, only to accept there are different ones out there.

- Learn the power of body language and how it impacts your presentation and your interactions.

- Consider completing a personal S.W.O.T. (Strengths, Weaknesses, Opportunities and Threats).

  Understanding where your strengths can combat your weaknesses and where your weaknesses can be used to create opportunity will give you the start of a practical life or career plan.

- The best way to make something new stick is to teach others, so create peer-to-peer mentoring groups, advocate for a Toastmasters group (skills work great for presentations and talking to customers), invite other departments to come to share about their work and send members of your team to other departments to do the same.

- Plan some department cross training, so peers learn how their work interacts with and impacts one another, while they build better relationships.

- Offer your opinion and insights objectively, being mindful of why you wish to share them and be open to the views of others. Be confident to say; "we can agree to disagree" without it negatively influencing the objective of the relationship overall.

- Seek out and inwardly promote your gifts and talents. We all have some fantastic skills and abilities. Make sure you are edifying your own and remain open to learning where you would like to grow and develop next.

- Have your team complete career-based elevator speeches, "I help "X" by doing "X" and my passion is "X". Add in an "I am looking for mentorship in "X."" Adapted from Kevin Warren's L.I.F.E. Program.[xxxvi] This is so much better than "I'm an accounts payable clerk" type limiting language.

    - e.g., *"I process thousands of invoices from our suppliers and ensure prompt and efficient payment on time, every time." My passion is learning new languages and I am seeking a French conversation partner to help develop my skills."*

- Compliment and express gratitude to other people, it will make you feel good too. A contagious and beneficial side bonus of Appreciative Inquiry is you will find you are naturally seeking the positives in others outside of the workplace which improves all your relationships!

As you gain confidence in understanding the layers that build who you are and recognize the same complexity in others, you will find yourself adjusting your approach to different personalities in little ways that benefit the relationship. It always stumped me a little when managers interpreted a corporate equality or fairness policy as people were some sort of robot entity that could not be provided with any allowances to their uniqueness.

I don't believe it is "fair" to paint every magnificently unique human with the same brush. Layer on personalities, learning styles, cultural nuances, mental health complexities, and you require slight shifts in your approach and interactions to attain the best possible version of each individual.

Of course, you do need to have parameters that align with the corporate culture and legal standards. From these starting points, you can discuss with your team a fair and consistent practice that maintains appropriate boundaries and sets of exception criteria to support trust with your team(s).

Your team need not know that someone is going through a challenging personal situation, managing a mental health concern, being performance managed, struggling with illness etc.... What your staff can understand is there is a list of circumstances that dictate some difference in duties and attention. For all to trust they will be given the same treatment respectfully should one of those identified issues arise for them.

There is also the element of Personality Styles in understanding others. I believe Personality Typing is an excellent self-development and leadership tool. There are many programs out there, with varying complexities, appropriate to different organizational levels and responsibilities.

You may already have one that your organization uses, or you can find them online. I teach three different versions depending on whether the client is executive/senior leadership, or for department teams or customer experience training, the last two being very simple, amusing, and easy for anyone to remember.

Why is understanding each other's personalities important? The stringent analytical staff will not take too kindly to a leader who perches on the side of their desk and wants to chat about personal weekend activities at length. However, the super outgoing employee will feel ignored if you never share a personal exchange. How can you treat everyone the same and manage to respect their particular manner of building and maintaining trusting relationships?

Relationships are at the core of workplace culture, whether Manager, Supervisor, Employee, or internal and external Client. It is beneficial to coach and mentors our teams understanding of personality and communication styles.

Also, to walk the talk in our interactions with them as we are teaching them to communicate better among themselves and with those they serve in business. For basic team building, personality typing helps develop robust employee engagement.

Your team will know why you are catching up on how your kids did in Football over the weekend with Sophia because her personality is suited to that personal interaction. You are admiring the organization skills of Stephen because that's what makes him glow with pride. You may "high-five" Tammy because she led an excellent focus group and her results were superior, and she wants to make sure you recognize that for her upcoming review.

Later, you stop by and chat with Peter, who gets a respectful nod and muted appreciation for his error-free excel spreadsheet because knowing he was precise in his work is what incentivizes his effort. A final stop to Eldon to say hello quietly while asking that he review his report in the *Grammarly.App* to fix some errors. As he very shy, quiet, and embarrassed about being dyslexic you offer him the night managers office to fix the report quietly.

From the outside perspective you spoke about different things with different body language and mannerisms, are you treating everyone differently? Yes. Are you treating everyone fair? Yes, by respecting their motivations and receptive styles. Everyone understands what you are doing and why and they know to utilize those same skills in their interactions.

No one will know why Eldon went into the office, but they will understand, based on the parameters of the team. They will appreciate that each of them has been given space in there for a personal issue or a specific deadline, so it isn't favoritism it is something falling within the known parameters of treatment. They trust in the process of fair and consistent leadership which, along with Appreciative Inquiry is an excellent start to enjoying very engaged teams.

For people-centered roles I love to teach Ego State management, the epic answer to managing conflict issues, leading objective based conversations, negotiating, and influencing. What happens when that calm, quiet co-worker loses their temper? The client is agitated, and you need to de-escalate them. You are having a challenging leader-subordinate conversation. You want to make the sale to or manage a moody customer?

It takes more than personality styles to have masterful interactive communications, especially with someone we don't have time to personality type. Dr. Eric Berne's Transactional Analysis[xxxvii] describes Ego States which are the results of the combined emotional inputs from nature and nurture plus personal growth and development when we interact with one another.

They are:

Parent – The parent represents the mass of data recorded in the brain from external events experienced from approximately 0-5 years of age. It is called the Parent State as that is the largest input during this stage of life but can include input from other adult and authority figures. It is called the Parent Ego State as it is the "taught" input recorded with no understanding of how to filter or edit the data as it comes in. A child does not yet know how to analyze and create their own perspective yet, so all information is imposed.

Child – The child state represents the brain recordings of internalized events and nature-based reactions to the external events the child is exposed to. This is the emotional, raw, real, natural aspect of our selves. How we feel when we are dealing with external stimuli. These are also recorded from 0-5 on average.

Adult – The Adult state is the last to develop. Around 1-2 years children begin to gain control over their body, expressions, and interactions. The brain starts to assess the data received and validate what is different between what they are told, what they observe and what they felt. Berne describes the Adult as being "principally concerned with transforming stimuli into pieces of information, and processing and filing that information on the basis of previous experience"[xxxviii]

EGO STATES	NATURAL/ADAPTIVE CHILD EGO STATE	PARENT EGO STATE	ADULT EGO STATE
WE ALL HAVE EACH THAT RISE UP BASED ON THE TRIGGER AND PERSON	A MIX OF NATURE AND NURTURE HOW WE REACT WHEN EMOTIONALIZED	INFLUENCED BY MATCHING AND MIRRORING ADULTS AROUND US. HOW WE BEGIN TO "PARENT" PETS, TOYS, OTHERS	REASONING BASED ON ALL INPUTS AND OWN INTERPRETATIONS
AGE	BIRTH - AGE 5	BIRTH - AGE 5	TALKING THROUGH ADOLESCENCE
INFLUENCE	THE "FELT" CONCEPT • HOW WE INTERNALIZE THE INPUTS AROUND US FROM A "FEELING" PERSPECTIVE. • IT IS OUR MOST NATURAL INNER EMOTIONAL STATE.	THE "TAUGHT" CONCEPT • HOW WE INTERNALIZE ALL THE STIMULI FROM THOSE IN POWER AROUND US. • THIS TEACHING IS BASED ON OBSERVING AND MIMICKING OUR PARENTS, GUARDIANS, CAREGIVERS, AND ADULT INFLUENCERS.	THE "THOUGHT" CONCEPT • AS EXPOSED TO NEW ADULTS, CHILDREN, MEDIA. • THIS IS HOW WE ASSESS WHAT WE KNOW AND BEGIN TO FORM OUR OWN LOGIC AND REASONING. • THIS IS WHERE OUR RATIONAL AND RESPONSIBLE SELVES SETTLE.

Dr. Harris a PhD student of Dr. Berne's created an easy summary that allows us quick understanding. In Dr. Harris's book "I'm OK, You're OK. he described the adult state as, *"a data-processing computer, which grinds out decisions after computing the information from three sources: the Parent, the Child, and the data which the adult has gathered and is gathering"*[xxxix]

In our training, we break these down into subcategories and go into this science a lot deeper by explaining how these Ego States get provoked and lead to ineffective communications and how to turn that around.

One of the biggest takeaways commonly shared in this section is people will revisit every challenging conversation they have ever had with new insight and a huge *"ah-ha ... so THAT's what went wrong there!"*

It is also fascinating that this communication science bridges the global and cultural differences common in any workplace today. Like body language, the result of neuroscience is common among all people, all cultures. I will share that there is no right or wrong ego state. We have all three styles when emotionalized and use them in different conversational situations, with different people and groups of people.

The science goes further to detail specific repeated patterns or scripts we fall into with certain personality types or groups. Perhaps you have had the experience of that one family member that seems to get into the same argument every holiday with the same person. When we are emotionalized, the topic is important to us, or we are triggered we will react in specific predictable and at times patterned in unpredictable ways.

These reactive communications do not always align perfectly with the personality typing with which we have been labelled. Which is why we can look at someone and say, *"Where did THAT reaction come from?"*

I had studied a lot of psychology and brain science for both self-development and to grow as a coach and leader before learning all this. At the time, my role was one of a Project Recovery Expert and Project Manager mentor. Often, the critical failure issues were related to insufficient or failing communications with the stakeholders, poor change management planning and usually ineffective management of their indirect project team members. I had reviewed and tested communications courses, presentation skills workshops, emotional intelligence, and personality style training.

All had positive impacts, however, failed to make the measurable differences I was seeking. Project Managers are often brilliant from an analytical, technical and process perspective; however, their people management skills are not usually as well developed. The Operational leadership they were serving were often A-type personalities with teams that required excellent communication and change management strategies for new initiatives.

When issues caused problems in the project it was often stress in the relationship between the project and operational areas that created the most significant failure points. The operational leadership lost interest and patience for the methodical slow, step by step processes as their focus shifted to getting things done, without causing more negative influence on their workgroups.

Over and over tensions were drilled down to when the project manager remained stuck to a process mindset and did not cultivate relationships or provide the communications needed to ease over issues. The staff or people impacted by the project outcome would be experiencing stress from any change coming their way.

Staff need a well-designed change and communication plans to remain engaged and productive during any operational change. Resistance and even sabotaging behaviors arise when people feel powerless and uninformed.

Understanding and working with different personalities remains quite manageable so long as everything is going smoothly. The clash tends to materialize when stressors come into play that ignite emotionalized interactions. People's emotional reactions didn't always match up to their known personality style. Dr. Eric Berne's Ego State Theory provides the logical understanding of why, which is why I teach both personality profiles and ego states in any team-based training.

This is not only a project management issue. Thinking back to my time as a senior manager in both operational and customer experience I recalled the same impacts and team issues. Further reflection confirmed that this was equally common in all our relationships both work and personal. I could mentor improvements in people skills but that took time and when you are rescuing a multi-million-dollar project, time is not a luxury provided.

Finally, one training program brought it all together for me. It was designed for the banking industry by James MacNeil and over time blended the Emotional Intelligence with leading-edge Communications strategies and win-win negotiation and influence psychology and philosophy. It was in the mix of learnings that those taking it made huge strides forward in people management understanding. The results were why I choose to become a Global Partner and build variations of this program to meet the needs of the common issues many leaders faced.

One of the lessons I learned was personality typing was important in team development, but as soon as stress arose, people reacted differently, and now I know why.

Ego States are a blend of nature (personality) and nurture (environmental inputs) and that is what makes us all so very unique when emotionalized in any way.

Building relationships with our teams provides results as there is no one size fits all in people management. By understanding ourselves and others using this neuroscience, we expand our Emotional Intelligence strengths by learning to control ourselves and our reactions far better. We will manage interactions and turn difficult or escalating conversations around and influence objective-based communication.

For a little more in-depth understanding of how soft skills impact our productivity and effectiveness at work, here is some insight into the neuroscience of emotions that feed our Ego States. Richard Davidson, Ph.D., Author of "Emotional Life of your Brain"[xl] wrote that our emotional styles comprise of six dimensions that build on the modern neuroscience research, they are:

- **Resilience: how slowly or quickly you recover from adversity.**

- **Outlook: how long you can sustain positive emotion.**

- **Social Intuition: how adept you are at picking up social signals from the people around you.**

- **Self-Awareness: how well you perceive bodily feelings that reflect emotions.**

- **Sensitivity to Context: how good you are with regulating your emotional responses within the context you face.**

- **Attention: how sharp and clear your focus is.**

Soft skills training that aids understanding in these skills will help build upon your Emotional Intelligence and interaction savvy. I layer these insights into workshops to give depth and meaning to why these skills are quite frankly, not "soft" at all; they are critical.

Outstanding leaders go out of the way to boost the self-esteem of their personnel. If people believe in themselves, it's amazing what they can accomplish.
~Sam Walton, Founder, Walmart

CHAPTER 12

INQUISITIVENESS ~ THE SECRET TO POSITIVE CHANGE

Curiosity is one of the permanent and certain characteristics of a vigorous intellect.
~Samuel Jackson

Take a moment to consider all the changes you have witnessed in your lifetime. From technological, environmental, political, social etc. very little could be described as it was 20, 40, 60 or 80 years ago. Change is our only constant, yet so many have negative associations surrounding this natural and evolving aspect of humanity. How does change happen? With curiosity!

Someone had an idea to make something better, faster, farther reaching, or different. Innovation is rarely the creation of something entirely new; it is often a redesign or improvement on something already in existence.

Much of our operational *"changes"* are more aptly named evolutions; sometimes the words we use can help ease an unfavorable response. Saying to your team "the system we are using for XYZ is going to be obsolete due to ABC. Therefore, we are evolving towards this model which looks awesome. A training plan is required, and I am requesting input on how you prefer to train for this updated system so we can accommodate all learning styles".

Consider the use computers and apps to resonate with generational readers. Consider the Baby Boomers and early GenX in clerical fields as they went through a massive shift from manual or electric assisted devices to black and green computer processors to the complexity of software programs today. It is one of the most significant advances in the adaptation of how to do a job that a workforce has experienced. Much of the same impact could be said for mechanics and others working in automation-based roles.

As an example, I learned about computers when a Major in the Military came into the room, zeroed in on me in the corner working background and investigative files for Intelligence. He came up and dumped 20 pounds of MS-DOS and UNIX books on my desk with a thud. He barked "you're the youngest one in here, we are getting computers a week Monday, read up, you will program them and teach the others." One does not reply *"the administration group supervisor is over there"* to a Major in the Armed Forces; one replies, *"yes sir"* and complies. The Administration Sergeant came over had a look and said, *"better you than me"* and walked away, and so goes delegation in the Military.

Curious, I opened up the MS-DOS book and a few pages in I was fascinated, there was a whole new technology and way of working, and I was at the forefront of learning it. After taking a peek, I would have been disappointed if it had been redirected to the correct person. In the meantime, it was mine to learn, and I was eager to embrace something new, it was exciting! In the Military, you do as you're told.

My nature was to embrace challenges and anything new as exciting and while my attitude helped me become the first female to achieve certain positions, it wasn't really required for success. As I moved into a civilian leadership role, I quickly learned I was an exception in this area. People no longer just did as they were told, and I quickly learned that most were not fond of change or challenge.

Nowadays, I could learn a new program every week and still feel like a dinosaur; there is so much to know. For many, from any generation, the pace of App development and software options is mind-numbing, and it can cause hesitation and overwhelm. The social expectation to be on the leading edge of what is new and emerging takes an incredible mental effort to stay on top of and comprehend well. The feeling of being overwhelmed is epidemic among young and old alike. When we hear change fatigue, we can do so with some understanding. It is why building resilience and adaptability becomes so imperative for a healthy workplace.

My son, who is in university, calls me to help him navigate the internet and software programs for his research work for essays and projects. He feels so pressured at times, in his effort to achieve the highest results and know everything, that his natural Ego State response is withdrawal, he shuts down and zones out on Vine and YouTube. That is true of many. The choice of how to zone out may change generationally, but it's the same action for the same reason. His core personality and predominate Ego State do not feel the excitement of constant discovery and learning unless it falls under his narrowly defined category of worthy topics to know and invest his time.

He is the typical "A" type personality that wants to be a perfectionist from the start so investing in learning takes enormous effort and dedication (he gets it from his Dad's side :D). Kidding - I am a wee bit guilty of that as well.

We all want to be knowledgeable in areas where it counts for us individually and collectively. More so though, by nature and nurture, I am invigorated by challenges and learning and have an *"opportunity and lessons learned"* mindset that developed during a difficult childhood. My son did not have that environmental input or experience to build upon. Unfortunately, like many of my GenX peers, I had a strong drive to make his childhood experience exceptional.

Both his father and I fell into the helicopter parenting role to ensure he did not suffer any of the misfortunes that I did, and his father wanted him to exceed in his options and opportunities as well. In retrospect, we did not do him any favors, and he now has to catch up and learn as a young adult.

Much the same as the majority of our Millennial and GenY folks are learning from their workforce experiences. It is an influencer to why I am so passionate about the training we do, the ah-ha lightbulbs that go off in our workshops and the thankful hugs at the end of a course make every event worthwhile. More than ever, this critical soft skill knowledge is needed.

There is nothing right or wrong about personality traits; they are what they are. Then we add the Ego States for emotionalized and reactive situations. Layer on the neuroscience of interactions and our natural learning intelligence and we get our unique imprint. All of these layered elements are learnable skills that significantly influence how a person succeeds in life, yet they are not taught in schools or workplaces with any consistency.

We have an unbalanced system where those who have *"born with it"* traits succeed with ease and resilience while others struggle with change and adaptation. This evolves into change fatigue and negatively impacts their wellness within their workgroups or school groups.

I sincerely wish *"I knew then what I know now"* about emotional intelligence, neuroscience, and appreciative inquiry methods. I would have been much better equipped in teaching the psychological underpinnings of excitement for change to my child and built up his emotional intelligence and resilience to better prepare him for a quickly evolving world. My son has taken our training, and the maturity and self-confidence that has come from it ease my mind that he is now much better prepared for the workforce he is about to enter.

If I could wave a magic wand, I would have this type of training from elementary schools onward and a mandatory part of every workplace on-boarding program.

We have talked about nature and nurture quickly so for the parents out there I will add one more tidbit; please build a sense of curiosity in your children, promote new learning and understanding as broadly as you can. It will help them when they enter an ever-evolving workforce.

My Grandfather, the Mayor of a small town for many years, used to walk almost daily and talk to folks. A couple of weeks during the summer that I spent with him are my most cherished memories because of what I learned. I would go with him as a child, and after almost every conversation we walked on, and he would say; *"now; I didn't know that" "well that was interesting,"* or *"people have great ideas when you take the time to ask."*

Unlike every other adult I knew he never told me to stop asking questions, he had limitless patience. He taught me to embrace my curiosity and seek the hidden bits of gold in others by always wondering what I was going to learn from them. He shared his popularity power secret of asking questions to gain intelligence and wisdom while making others feel good. It was one of my most valuable childhood lessons and served me well in my leadership roles.

The more you grow your relationships with others through Appreciative Inquiry, the more rapport and influence you develop with your teams and the higher the employee engagement among them. Influencing a positive environment of curiosity allows for smoother transitions during change initiatives.

My confidence in leading others came from understanding the value in a team, learned from my Military experience, and developed in every role I undertook. I knew *"if I was the lone voice of ideas, innovation or change in the room, there was a problem."*

Not because I lack intelligence or confidence in my ideas, but due to the fact we are stronger, smarter, and more capable when all opinions, ideas and processes are worked through from various viewpoints. Surrounding yourself with *"mini-me's"* will not provide the innovative, strategic, and thorough outcomes we strive for in excellence. When you develop your questioning skills in every meeting and performance conversation, the expectation and acceptance of ideation and change planning will become second nature to the entire team. No more *"change fatigue!"*

Sustainable capacity for change and marketplace evolution requires a consistent effort to disrupt stagnate thinking. The way of yesterday is in the past, and an agile workforce is created when forward-thinking, inquisitive environments are cultivated.

When I work with a client on Strategic Planning, I start with disruptive systems thinking, using tools like the Business Model Canvas to delve into their business as if it were an upstart. I use the 6-Hats thinking exercise to open up the planning teams' minds to planning for the future from a big picture inquiring perspective. Both shake up the tired standard of strategic planning I often see.

An inquiry mindset is the seed of change because it brings the mental question of *"what if?"*

- *"What if we could harness new technology to serve our clients better, in half the time and extend your focus on other, more important tasks? What would you want to spend more time accomplishing?"*

- *"What if we offer new customers a 10% discount when they sign with us and at the end of the sales call, we ask them if there were anything different, they would like to maintain their loyalty?"*

- *What if we polled our customers service calls to include "on a scale of 1-10 how did we make you feel by the end of our call?" rather than how they "think" it went or whether the agent served them well. (Hint: Brand Booster)*

- *What if we asked our employees/peers/departmental counterparts the following questions regularly and whatever they said we responded: "thank you for sharing that with me, I appreciate understanding your perspective."*

- *"What if we could tear apart ABC work and start from scratch, what would make this process better?"*

- *"What if process and rules/legislation were removed, is there a way we could improve our client/process interactions or outcomes?"*

- *"What if you could influence a happier, more enjoyable work environment, what would you adjust or change?"*

> *Creative disruption addresses both the technical and human elements of change by building an organization-wide capability in inquiry, listening, and collaborative problem-solving.*
> *~Mark Dillard*

When your team feels like they are valued, that their opinions matter, your engagement skyrockets. Bringing Emotional Intelligence and Appreciative Inquiry to the workplace is not about being touchy-feely; it is about growing an innovative, resilient, agile team that is prepared to adapt productively to anything coming their way.

We can all ask a question that seeks to source a variety of thinking. When different types of "thinkers" come together, it can create various inputs to changes that can alter how we view many things in our lives. Leading dozens of teams over the years, I learned early on that a good question can create a better plan, a better outcome, and a more engaged employee.

> *As a leader, if I am the smartest person in the room, there's a problem with the team I've put together.*
> *~Deirdre von Krauskopf*

When we bring together different personality types, diverse expertise and then open up *"cloud"* thinking in the early stages of planning, we get the broadest scope of ideas and far-reaching impacts, innovation flourishes. Change is embraced because your teams are part of the solution and not just the end users of what is downloaded to them.

In an Innovation Excellence article by Mukesh Gupta titled *"Innovation starts with a Question,"*[xli] he shares a great questioning technique that I encourage you to research and learn. He states. **"In a world where it is challenging to sustain any competitive advantage you build, it is essential to continually innovate and come up with new ideas, products, and solutions and that too, at speed. We all know that innovation always starts with insight. You have an insight when you suddenly see things differently. You see things differently when you start looking at things differently. You start looking at things differently when you are trying to answer a different question. You can trace most innovations and creative endeavors to a question that someone asked. It all starts with a question. The question that you ask is what determines the kind of answers you get. So, if you ask bad questions, you will get bad answers. If you ask good questions, you might get good answers. However, if you ask interesting questions, you get interesting answers, and in my opinion, interesting answers are better than good answers."**

Your Staff Gravitates Towards What is Expected of Them

When you look at a job opening on a recruitment site, what type of posts capture your eye first? It is likely you gravitate to the ones that mention your kind of skill set.

You feel confident reading these posts first because you know what they are asking for, they fall within your area of expertise, and you're sure you can do the job because you know what will be expected of you.

In a workgroup people excel when they understand what is expected of them, know their measured goals and how they contribute to the larger picture. The same effect is real for anyone. When you are transparent with your expectations, staff are more apt to perform intentionally and productively.

When we lead with a positive mindset and an open, curious attitude we create an environment of innovation expectation through our actions. Your employees naturally want to participate when we encourage them to feel the same way and create an atmosphere of acceptance to different concepts and ideas.

With consistent practice, your team will evolve toward an agile, innovative, and adaptable mindset as those become common expectations. The new "norm" encourages growth, learning and curiosity which enables a more positive, upbeat, and confident outlook towards change and business evolution.

Your team begins to think more critically about HOW they do things and for what outcome. They will build self-esteem when their insights are heard, understood, accepted, and respected, and that will naturally gravitate individuals towards improved communications and relationship management.

When I was tasked *"to fix"* a series of negative, low engaged workgroups, it was usually with a quiet nod towards *"someone,"* the senior management thought needed to be fired to turn around the group.

The first thing I initiated in any 30-60-90-day plan was to establish expectations that included a team that shared information and ideas freely and was respected by peers when doing so. The next was to develop workgroup norms and a shared understanding towards our department objectives, so we were all speaking the same language. It was always an enlightening meeting to hear the variations of understanding folks had about one strategic sentence or objective.

Lastly, I made it clear that in my first 30 days I wanted to resolve outstanding issues and confusion and that required them to be willing to share, even if they didn't *"feel"* I wanted to hear it. Employees must feel comfortable raising concerns and bringing you problems; it is part of leadership. If they don't trust you enough to take their interests seriously, you will end up with a malcontent workgroup in no time.

Few leaders are taught to set out the culture and environment they aspire to manage and then hold themselves accountable to that expectation through leading by example.

Individually, I would then meet with each person. These meets were not in my office but by their side at their workstation to learn what they did in real time while I built a rapport with them. The #1 comment I received, from multiple organizations, was *"no Manager has ever taken this kind of interest in what I do."*

With a connection that wasn't overtly authority to subordinate starting the relationship, you would be surprised at how people opened up after an hour or two and began their journey towards a better team environment. So those *"troubled employees"*? They, like all of us, had a story to share and like every human interaction, there is more than one side to the story.

What I learned was that far too often they grew into their negative attitudes through mixed, unknown, or continually changing expectations. Often this led to clashing personalities with their leader. Once they knew what they were expected to do and WHY it contributed importantly to the outcome of the organization's strategic objective, they felt part of the journey.

When they accepted that I was willing to press restart and value their expertise and experience as long as they moved towards the new team culture it seemed like a visible burden had been lifted from their shoulders. More often than not someone who had been *"targeted"* to be fired turned around and became productive, contributing members of the team. My consistent ability to turn workgroups around and to achieve record gains in employee opinion surveys often led to my teaching and mentoring other leaders.

> *Leadership involves solving problems.*
> *The day subordinates stop bringing you their issues is the day you have stopped leading them. They have either lost confidence that you can help or concluded you do not care. Either case is a failure of leadership.*
> ~Colin Powell

Practical Illustration

Allen was a negative influence in a workgroup and had been labelled as a troublemaker. He was in the midst of escalating performance reviews; his job dissatisfaction was apparent and seeping into his teammates in toxic ways. Julie, the new Manager, was told going in that Allen had one more chance and he was to be terminated.

Julie had recently taken the High-Performance Team Building Leadership Workshop that included Appreciative Inquiry, so she was well prepared for her arrival and spent time reviewing his and the other's files. She noticed the vast differences in performance reviews from the 13 different managers holding this position over the past eight years. It seemed that issues were personality or behavior based in many circumstances.

It appeared Allen did not have high emotional intelligence and would react defensively and angrily when his intentions were questioned. He also did not seem well trained in dealing with difficult people, so his escalated customer interactions did not go well.

In conversation with the team, she could feel the apathy as she began to introduce her style of leadership. So, she stopped, mid-sentence and paused a moment before asking "take me through the basics here, what do we do and why?" This tactic seemed to shock some, and then Allen piped up and said: *"you're the manager, shouldn't you be telling us that."*

Rather than bristle at his response she replied *"I would prefer to lead a team by understanding your jobs through your eyes, understanding how you see your contribution in serving our customers and how I can best support you in that goal. You've all been here a long time, and I would like to honor and respect your expertise as we build a team culture together."*

The team stirred with interest and one by one; they slowly shared what they did and how they contributed. The spark grew as Julie probed what impeded their best success and what they wanted in her as a leader. Perhaps a little uncomfortable for some but the responses she did receive matched her awareness that every previous Manager had a new way of doing things to make their mark, and it caused confusion and tension.

Everyone wanted to do a good job and be acknowledged for it; the basics are usually that simple in a workgroup. This one simple line of questioning opened up further conversations on how they should better their service overall, and to everyone's surprise, Allen seemed to be reinvigorated, introducing idea after idea.

When Julie was doing her introductory one on ones with each member, Allen started with *"I guess you have seen my file and are aware I'm the problem child here."* Julie shared that yes, she had reviewed the files however there seemed a disconnect from the enthusiasm and notable expertise he displayed in their recent meeting. She asked him directly *"I liked what I saw in that meeting, what do you need from me to show the team more of that?"*

Allen paused awhile and then said, *"I'm not sure, no one has ever asked me that before."*

Julie said, *"I would like to help you achieve your goals for the future rather than focus on your past. You have been given some insight into how I want to lead and that my expectations are a united culture working towards common goals in a pleasant and respectful environment. That is going to include some personal development training for everyone to aid their interactions with customers and each other.*

Can I count on your willingness to share your experience and expertise with the newer team members when we do team exercises and build our communication skills? Give it some thought this weekend and let's talk on Monday about where you see how best to contribute and what you would like to attain for your future. Then we can discuss how we can make that happen." He looked at her directly and said, *"the fact that you care enough to ask is a good start."*

The following week they had a planning session, set his performance goals and expectations and to everyone's surprise, a different version of him was lit up and open to making a positive difference. After the workshop, it still took some mentoring and guidance. Like any new skill set once learned, it takes consistent practice to build expertise.

In a few short months, Allen completely turned around, and eventually became a trainer and stand in as the supervisor for the team. A valuable, experienced, knowledgeable change ambassador for the organization rather than a disengaged employee with a target on his back.

*The enterprise that does not innovate
inevitably ages and declines.
And in a period of rapid change
such as the present,
the decline will be far.*
~Peter Drucker

CHAPTER 13

DEVELOPING COACHABLE TEAMS

A leader takes people where they want to go.
A great leader takes people where they don't
necessarily want to go, but ought to be.
~ *Rosalynn Carter*

Leading any group of unique and diverse individuals can be a difficult task on its own. Coaching requires you to help them develop the best within themselves which can be a further challenge if they cannot or don't care to see the best within themselves.

There are distinct differences between managing, coaching, and mentoring someone and when we blur those roles, even with the best of intentions, we can come across as critical, negative, or parental. When we use Appreciative Inquiry, along with other coaching, mentoring and leadership strategies, we are developing and showing our team that it takes a toolbox of different skills to create success.

Finding a solution to any problem may require one or more approaches and the more open and adaptable we are in managing an issue using a broad scope perspective, the more likely we will find our solution. These are the coping skills that will create confident, innovative, and productive teams.

Managing with Appreciative Inquiry sets clear expectations for both performance and behavior to create a cohesive and positive culture among your team.

Coaching, however, in its purest form, is guiding the person to seek, define and bring forth the best version of themselves. This technique is a guiding and questioning process, not a mentoring or directive approach. As a good coach, you will lead them to their results with their best interest in mind.

Using Appreciative Inquiry questions, you will gain much further ground in bringing out the best in someone then through a directive approach, especially if the person is resistant to change. When someone moves towards an objective or change, feeling they are empowered in the process, the engagement is much higher.

The coaching questions I have found most helpful are based on core coaching questions learned at a 3-day Pure Coaching Certification Program that we can now include, as a preferred partner to all our leadership programs. With an objective defined, ask:

- **What do you want to achieve?**

- **What are you doing to attain your goals?**

- **How's that working for you?**

- **If there were no constraints, what would you do differently?**

- **What are you willing to commit to right now?**

Executives and HR managers know coaching is the most potent tool for inducing positive personal change, ensuring better-than-average odds of success, and making the change stick for the long term.
~ The Ivy Business Journal

Coach and Build Around What Works

When we examine how our business is running, we analyze what is working and what is not and adjust accordingly. We have an overarching Vision, Mission, and Strategy and then a series of plans to aid the success of the business.

These plans are likely reviewed and updated every 5-10 years or as market conditions require intermediate adjustments. As a leader, you will probably have an operational plan or workgroup plan that built around your contribution to the strategic plan. The key to coaching well-managed teams is developing understanding and contribution towards strategic objectives. This is best accomplished by engaging your team in the planning process and using the strengths and knowledge they bring to the table.

A team is always more involved if they feel part of the process and one way is encouraging their growth and sustainability through innovative ideas and pilots aimed at future change. This dynamic builds a subtle and constant process that will make any substantial change initiative easier to integrate.

Too often, as managers or leaders, change, planning is done in silos and rolled out in a manner that derails our employees from what they usually do by creating *"a better way"* without their input. Imagine how much that devalues their combined experience and knowledge and creates management-employee divides; no wonder change is resisted! I expect most planning sessions that fall under this example are undertaken with the best of intentions. However, it will likely lead to disengagement, unfounded rumors, work slowdowns and stoppages and overall delays and hindrance to the process.

Consistent, or what I like to call evolving, operational processes come when you build constant change in the culture. You must first assess the current state, both operations and the employee's productivity. Then begin regularly asking questions that open possibilities, such as *"if there were no policy, procedural or legislated requirements how would you do your job differently?"* Another starter question is, *"If you could change anything about what you do to become more efficient or serve our clients better, what would it be?"*.

If more significant changes are needed, take the time to learn a change management process and plan the roll out with a few key members of your team as ambassadors. In my role at Regional Government, a few of us were certified as Change Management Professionals, with Prosci's ADKAR model[xlii].

Whenever I led operational, strategic or project initiatives I found incorporating the end user in the planning process and working as much of the current structure that made sense into the new direction helps ease the transition.

When people feel they are contributing and influencing their new roles they buy-in quicker and feel valued in the process. I have yet to work on a change plan that did not include a people element. ADKAR stands for:

Awareness   **- Business Need**
Desire   **- Concept and Design**
Knowledge   **- Implementation**
Ability   **- Implementation**
Reinforcement **- Post Implementation**

There are other change management models out there for you to research however, I like this one for ease of understanding by leadership and employees alike.

I also find that using Appreciative Inquiry helps in building a culture of expectant change. It starts with being consistent in meetings, coaching sessions and during performance expectation meetings, building the idea that change is a welcome constant. More as a continuous evolution to meet changing markets, clients' needs and personal development than *"a thing that happens to them."*

This consistency takes the "change fatigue" equation off the table as it becomes part of your culture to seek out innovation, "next practices," and new opportunities. Please connect with me if looking for more information on Change Management strategies.

Change is the law of life.
And those who look only to the past or present
are certain to miss the future.
~John F. Kennedy

Focus on Incremental Increases

Far too many managers lead with a focus on the negative task list. In our Team Building training, we have a leadership add-on that teaches the outstanding outcomes you can achieve when you place a stronger focus on the behaviors you want increased. Gains are realized through Appreciative Inquiry, understanding Ego States, and working on Emotional Intelligence with Advanced Communications Skills.

When we teach a baby to walk, we do not focus on how many times they fall. We encourage another effort and cheerlead every step forward accomplished. If we taught babies with focused attention on their failures, we could potentially have many children taking much longer to reach the developmental milestone of walking independently and, it doesn't change with age.

People succeed when given authentic encouragement, clear expectations with supportive mindsets. For Leadership, we expand our training of Ego States in a workplace environment and include Games People Play[xliii] from Dr. Eric Berne's work, and Drama Triangles[xliv] from one of his students, Dr. Stephen Karpman. This deeper dive teaches leadership assessment and response skills beyond the personality types, which are great when everything is running smoothly, but not as helpful when someone is responding on an emotional level.

Understanding the psychology of how people are triggered or why they seem to overreact to the way you present something is an eye-opening experience for many. Our training provides an opportunity for skill development in learning to control your message to meet your objectives, managing interactions to gain success, as well as de-escalating and influencing others to calm them and to encourage proactive and productive mindsets. I cannot emphasize enough that, when you have a predominant or a singular focus on decreasing specific areas, such as mistakes, lack, attitude, tardiness and complaints, our subconscious is *"primed"* to see the negative attributes of the person.

Continue along this path too long, and you will find yourself automatically attuned to a regular negative mindset that it will be hard to find something the person does *"right."* This is equally important to recognize in those personal relationships that matter the most to you, with significant others, children, other family, and friends.

> *If you don't like something, change it.*
> *If you cannot change it,*
> *change the way you think about it*
> *~Mary Engelbreit*

Have you ever bought a new car that you felt was somewhat unique only to start seeing it everywhere you drive? Is it a coincidence? No. You are experiencing *"frequency illusion,"* also known as the Baader-Meinhof phenomenon.

Stanford linguistics professor Arnold Zwicky coined the term in 2006 to describe the syndrome. He writes, *"My original posting connected the phenomenon to two well-known cognitive biases in psychology. Selective attention (once you've noticed something, you are more attentive to occurrences of it than you were before) and confirmation bias (in which you're inclined to collect instances of the phenomenon, as confirming your hypothesis about its frequency, and discount the many disconfirming instances in your experience)."xlv*

Therefore, the Emotionally Intelligent leader cognitively focuses on what aspects should be improved. Keeping a focus on what is done well before noting an area of development, ensures appropriate consideration of the person's positive contributions of the job first. Then should coaching or mentoring be required, use the Appreciative Inquiry questioning technique, to influence their acknowledgement of an issue and their offered corrections. Finish with an acknowledged appreciation for their ownership and commitment to change.

Should some coaching be required to gain some mutual understanding of an area of potential, you approach the employee with what we call an "open-directed" question that is not critical of the individual and focused on their thoughts on a situation. This approach keeps the onus on the employee to offer up a solution or if required, choose a preferred option.

An example would be *"what options would you suggest building greater confidence and proficiency in ABC?"*

Alternatively, *"Would you prefer Max, Jocelyn or Tyrell on your team to assist the lagging statistical research?"* Giving options to move towards the expectations you have set gives them a feeling of empowerment over their performance and greater acceptance of a required performance improvement.

This style of leadership was one of the reasons for my successes when taking over low performing or critical workgroups and turning them around. Even those employees who were identified as problem employees had notable skills in some areas, often overlooked. Maintaining my primary focus on where they contributed well and following up using open-directed questions that allowed self-directed adjustments, I empowered those labelled troublemakers to turn crashing careers around with dignity.

I am not recommending that you ignore or minimize serious performance issues, however. Setting clear expectations for both performance and behavior in both one-on-one and group settings will ensure someone won't feel segregated and picked on. Document every conversation, choices offered, and commitments made, anticipating this effort will aid a much-improved performance review.

Alternatively, for the few times you are unable to turn someone around, it provides you with clear documentation for a continuous performance improvement plan. You are offering your employee a clean slate in your mind while holding them and your team accountable, which allows them a belief that their past can be overcome.

Can you remember a time where you wished you could have had a *"do-over"* or an opportunity to reinvent yourself and change how someone perceives you? By focusing on and encouraging their positive attributes, you are giving this gift, and you will be surprised how many *"bad employees"* turn around.

Encourage performance improvements in different areas:

- **A sales or client service call that went well**
- **Acts of service or kindness**
- **Productivity gains, no matter how small**
- **Appreciation and respect for their tenured experience or expertise**
- **Innovative ideas and suggestions offered in a positive way**
- **When they recognize the good work of others.**

> *The thing that lies at the foundation*
> *of positive change, the way I see it,*
> *is service to a fellow human being.*
> *~Lee Iacocca, past CEO, Chrysler*

Often when we stop and listen to how people speak of one another, there is a tendency to focus on the critic. What was wrong with that person or what we didn't like about another. As I mentioned earlier regarding my grandfather, who repeatedly won elections with landslide wins, he taught me that without people to lead there was no leader.

He made an effort to meet everyone who wanted some of his time and probed people until he a found a connection with them. He would also offer unique compliments, something about them that stood out to him. He was highly respected and very well loved by all. I emulated that in my professional career by always seeking the good, the interesting and that unique compliment that could be said with utmost authenticity and made the person feel special.

As a mentor, coach, and leader I would focus on the best someone had to offer and then coach them in areas of improvement. I also asked for feedback and worked to be a better manager for them. Showing that self-improvement was a two-way street, and we were better together when building a better team. It is a beneficial aspect of being generally positive when you allow yourself to see the best in people instead of being critical. You will usually find they respond much better when change is required.

Of course, no one is perfect, and we all have some area that could use improvement, but that doesn't mean we have to be defined by it. When we recognize the best in people, not only do we benefit from knowing what great attributes they can contribute, but it makes the employee more empowered and self-confident with their role.

Confident employees tend to perform better, work more creatively and be significantly more engaged in the expected outcomes. Don't be afraid to compliment employees on their job skills and what they have accomplished, even when, or especially when they have performance concerns. Be as specific as possible on what you like. Make it unique and personable.

Detail a strengths profile on their excellent qualities alongside a development required list and then determine which list overpowers the other before deciding on follow up actions, so you are managing or coaching with the right context and frame of mind.

> *Positive thinking will let you do everything better*
> *then negative thinking will.*
> ~ Zig Ziglar

Limit or Remove Negative Comments

Creating a negative relationship with discouraging phrases and terms is one of the leading influences on poor behavior, lacking performance and low morale. Harsh or harmful words can damage any employment relationship and can usually bring out a sense of defensiveness when approached. Once said or written, the person is often hyper-focused on that criticism and cannot hear anything else.

When we teach any people focused workshop, we include neuroscience segments. There are easy to understand psychological triggers on how emotions are evoked. When we approach others in a caustic or controlling manner that flairs their critical ego state, we provoke fear, pride, or confusion. That is incredibly ineffective if our objective is to create a positive or productive change in someone.

Once we have flared their defense mechanism in one of

these categories, it is doubtful they will be positively open to hearing anything you have to say, let alone respect your leadership. They may be afraid of you or the power you have to impact their employment negatively, but employees that are fearful or angry can do a lot of underhanded damage to your team, your customers, and your reputation. It is also how poisonous or toxic workplaces often begin.

When you find yourself wanting to use challenging or negative phrases, either with your internal self-talk or with others, stop and think of the words you're using. Then rethink the sentence by removing negative comments and replacing them with a positive framing aimed towards the change you want to see. You will find that you can still get your point across without making the employee feel as though they are being attacked.

Often when you approach an issue with Appreciative Inquiry questions, they will see the mistake and feel more empowered to suggest and make corrections themselves.

*In every day, there are 1,440 minutes.
That means we have 1,440 daily opportunities
to make a positive impact.*
                              ~Les Brown

CHAPTER 14

IT STARTS WITH YOU!

I combine my emotional intelligence, experience and understanding of business with [good] coaching, and the result is magic.
~ *Tom Walter*

Be Coachable: Top Down / Peer-to-Peer / Bottom Up

It starts with you! If we expect our teams to be positive, accepting of change, and coachable, then we have to develop it within ourselves first and then present ourselves this way. Emotional Intelligence has been proven as a critical component of success from entry-level to C-level executives.

Sure, IQ and job-related skills are essential aspects of getting a job, but often the defining element of keeping a job and getting ahead has more to do with the soft skills, which are not usually part of any level of a school's curriculum. You can't expect it from others until you are leading by example.

Building a strong core of soft skills in yourself ensures that you can have the confidence you need to handle the changes and challenges at work and lead the way for others. Creating an environment where staff are rewarded for developing their wellness strategies, positivity and self-awareness ensure that coworkers can work optimally together.

Managing yourself internally can be very important to your ongoing success. Many "skills" can be found online these days. However, when it comes to communications, rapport, influence, any "people skills" we can all understand it's an interactive process, so better with experiential in-person training.

Coaching for Strengths

When being asked about coaching the wealthiest people in the world Lolly Daskal, Executive leadership coach to hundreds of millionaires and billionaires stated, ***"The secret to their success doesn't boil down to one specific habit, routine, or personality trait. The secret of the true billionaire is what's going on the inside. In other words, the secret to success starts with your own psychology — not the specific actions you take. You have to know who you are and what you want, and you have to continually challenge those notions before you can even begin to influence others."***

We give ourselves confidence when we have identified our strengths, as it reminds us of, and bolsters our spirit on what we do very well. We can then view what we are good at doing and when we get to the "what we need to work on."

It isn't as cynical; it's a work in progress. We have built up where we shine first, and the rest is a learning opportunity to improve. Self-education is a lifelong process. If we don't notice our strengths and are hypercritical, we may only focus on the things we do poorly. We can even assume that we don't have any valuable traits, or worse, downplay the ones we do have.

A great exercise to find our strengths includes making a list of things we are amazing at, things we are great at, even those we are good at if you want to get detailed and then list what we would like to improve on. I love to add a list that says, *"Danger, you suck at this, stay away"* to bring humor into it, of course, but also to remind myself I am not meant to be good at everything. We can all accept or believe that no one is masterful at everything.

Amazing Skills	Great skills	Want to Develop	Danger - I suck at this

The last column can be started with items that lighten things up a little or something obvious to you! I would list taxes and grammar proofing (thank you again Chris and

Donna), so I hire people for that! Start with one thing where you are indeed a danger to yourself or others. Such as, *"I have no interest in fixing mechanical equipment so, keep me away."* Alternatively, *"I am tone deaf and therefore not meant to be a musician."* This real but goofy insight will ease the pressure off those of you who have perfectionist streaks.

Once you release the obvious, you can relax the mind and focus on items that you want to improve rather than "I want to be great at everything." You may wish to use this as a peer exercise for team building because often other folks will honor our skills far higher than we may do ourselves.

Then for the items you wish to work on you have a group of people available to share their ideas, mentoring or offer up great coaches and resources to help you.

Creating a team accountability plan is an advanced phase tool for building career-enhancing skills and knowledge. Keep in mind that it may be a bit too much for some when beginning your team building journey.

For leaders that genuinely want to see dynamic changes in their team, allow your employees to contribute to your performance goals and commit to actions. This humbling method is one of the ways I turned around toxic workgroups fast, by leaving my Ego at the door and gathering their perspective on what they wanted to see from me, their leader.

Recognize that if you are new to the workgroup, you will be wearing the sins of every Manager before you for the first round or two. You will however soon be making rapid relationship gains and building trust by opening yourself to upward performance management.

Modify your list to align with the relevant areas of the corporate employee satisfaction survey. Your personal and workgroup marks will go up and so will the overall scores in areas you do not have direct control over.

Building a Trusting Team Coaching Environment

Leading by example will also improve acceptance of your employee's performance improvement plan. By having them complete this type of chart in advance, you will gain valuable insight on where they see themselves and where they want to go.

I would ask for it a week or so in advance so I had time to network and research areas that would help enhance their skills mentioned in their "develop my work section." It will also give you time for a considered response if their self-perception is at odds with your assessment.

A modified team version can be created for workgroup strength building through cross-training, preparing for new software or systems knowledge and succession planning, for example.

It fuels the concept of we are stronger, smarter, and more effective when we are a balanced group with "next generation" skills and abilities working towards common objectives. Expanding cross-training, peer mentoring and course approvals for non-job specific training will develop agile, adaptable, and more cohesive working teams. It also greatly assists cross-departmental collaboration and grows a collective expertise that is shared more freely. *"Break down the Silos!"*

When I do this modified team exercise in a workgroup setting, we make it a lot of fun. I request that each employee first add their self-assessment.

You may specify a number to be recorded, e.g., 4 in the first column, 3 in the next, 2 in what to develop. The "Danger, You Suck" column is removed for this sharing exercise as you don't want to make anyone feel uncomfortable.

This group exercise is best completed after other team building training has been completed and once a positive flow is created within your team. However, it can also be quite useful with a reasonably cohesive unit that is preparing for a change initiative. If you have a disengaged group keep this exercise to a mentoring and coaching environment one on one until the other tools in this book have developed a more positive team.

Have your team members find a partner to review their list. The partner is to add what they value most about the person, in both the first and second column. It allows teams to appreciate each other's skills and share how they see each other's contributions. It is often eye-opening to the person when they hear what other skills people value in them.

Leave it to each team member to specifically ask if they want further feedback in the "wants to improve column" to avoid any unnecessary adverse situations. Overall, this exercise maintains the positive focus and builds the idea that we have a range of skills that together creates a stronger, high performing team. You can use the outcome of this private or group exercise to define the Performance Review section that guides individual development. You may add that the employee reviews their list each month and indicates where or how they demonstrated this trait.

For the first two columns, it will give you excellent examples to make their reviews personal and value their contributions. For the third column, ask them to ponder what action they will take to improve upon it over the review period, and then you can track those personally motivated efforts.

In a unit that is deemed toxic or has been *"poisoned"* by bad leadership or team negativity, this exercise can still be done in a one-on-one setting to clarify expectations. It will help guide the individual towards the culture you are seeking. Some may gripe vocally at first, but when they have to evaluate their effort within their team's performance objectives and perhaps internal and cross-department collaboration they will self-adjust faster understanding that bigger picture.

When they have to put it in writing and monitor their actions and growth, it builds greater accountability and a shift in attitude for most employees.

Tips for finding strengths:

- **Analyze how you present yourself to others; are you leading by example?**

- **Determine what your growth objectives are and how you will move towards them.**

- **Examine the ways you solve problems, what works and what needs some attention.**

You may mentor and coach by listing the great and good attributes along with "needs work" and even add in a *"needs team assistance"* column.

Keep it a living performance tracking document and watch your team evolve with better self-mastery and team integration.

Best Practices

Sometimes, the term *"best practices"* can be confusing if we don't attach them to something. In Appreciative Inquiry, best practices refer to interaction practices that work best for your culture and the strategic goals of the company.

You can consider these questions when asking your team to build a workgroup culture of Appreciative Inquiry.

- What practices make you feel the most confident and positive?

- What practices make you feel you have contributed to team or organizational goals when you finish them?

- What practices improve employee morale and progress?

Remember best practices can be individualized to each person when mentoring and coaching. As we learned earlier on with personality and Ego State management, what resonates for one person may not resonate for another.

Individuals:

- What results would you want to see that give you the confidence that you did an outstanding job?

- What workplace habits do you enjoy that help you to stay on track with your workload?

- What aspects of your work make you feel positive about the end-result?

Peak Moments

Peak moments are times in which we feel the highest levels of happiness and possibility. They can happen in everyday situations or during extreme events in our lives. They can occur when we accomplish a new goal or finish a long project. They most often involve other people.

In the workplace, they can include a natural flow in great client interactions, attained deadlines we worked hard to achieve, being so focused that time flies by basically any outcome or situation where we feel felt a great sense of accomplishment without feeling pressure.

The key is to remember the lessons learned, what you can duplicate in the future, how the accomplishment made us feel positive and confident. While they are not necessarily "ah-ha" moments, we all have particular remembered experiences that stick with us, and we can recall how we felt when we experienced them. Have your team document these moments and keep them updated on a performance-based self-mastery list.

Celebrating Successes

Many times, our employees don't think about the excellent work they do every day. Whether they are modest, or it's never been a focus, it is a missed opportunity to develop better self-perception. To be fulfilled and happy at work we want to encourage self-confidence. Praise individual contribution and build team pride in achieving goals that contribute to the broader strategic objectives.

Our past successes are our foundation for building progress in our career development. By celebrating and documenting our accomplishments, we remind ourselves of all the achievements that went into attaining a goal. When we relive these successes, it can remind us that we can overcome almost anything and can feel ultimately better about ourselves and our success. It can reduce our stress and serve as an anchor for positivity.

All of us can think of a time when we were learning to do something for the first time, the challenge or even frustration. With a conscious thought, we can also recall when that feeling disappeared once we have mastered it.

For teams that need to work with other workgroups to achieve success, as well as supervisors and above, I highly recommend a 360 assessment. Many people's job success is dependent on the input and cooperation of other areas or levels. A two-way review of what is working and where support is required to improve can aid a team's success greatly.

DvK Partner Group administers 360 assessments with an Emotional Intelligence, Personality Typing and Ego State assessment. Three coaching calls are included for each employee assessed to ensure the results go beyond evaluations and provide the person with a clear action plan to move forward.

Individual Log for Remembering Successes

- **Keep a visual reminder such as a self-mastery list or achievement list to use for your review.**

- **Review these successes regularly. When taking on new work, review how you have achieved success in the past to set your mindset positively.**

- **Talk about achievements with your friends and peers, share and learn from each other.**

Practical Illustration

Robert was feeling depressed after his last presentation. He felt as though he didn't do his best work, as he usually does, and was feeling down about it.

Robert was determined his next presentation would be up to his old standards. First, he made a list of all his strengths and how he puts them to good use. Then he made notes of some ways his strengths help him reach his other goals.

He asked for positive feedback from trusted attendees and incorporated their thoughts into his records.

He visualized how these successes would benefit his future presentations. When he had his mindset fixed on all of his past accomplishments, he felt very confident in himself and thought he could do a better job on the next project. He was determined not to let one mishap deter him from succeeding next time.

*The greatest discovery of my generation
is that a human being can alter his life
by altering his attitudes*
　　　　　　　　　　~William Jame

♞ DVK PARTNER GROUP ♞
~YOUR STRATEGIC PARTNER IN TRAINING~

BUILD YOUR TEAM STRENGTH WITH
WORKSHOPS THAT TRANSFORM

UNIQUELY DESIGNED PROGRAMS
BUILT WITH A FOUNDATIONAL CORE OF:

ADVANCED COMMUNICATIONS,

NEUROSCIENCE, BODY SCIENCE

EMOTIONAL INTELLIGENCE, AND

RAPPORT BUILDING

INFO@DVKPARTNERGROUP.COM

I would love to serve your teams, please connect.

Share your thoughts and feedback to
info@DvKPartnerGroup.com

**Book your free consultation,
because your team is worth it**

1-844-333-7526

ABOUT THE AUTHOR

Deirdre von Krauskopf helps organizations achieve measurable and transformational change through the power of people. She utilizes a uniquely designed combination of self-mastery, neuroscience, and the leading human development advances. Her company partners with trainers across the Globe to offer wide-ranging subject matter expertise.

Deirdre weaves a core training success strategy into every course. The cornerstone being neuroscience, with the foundational aspects of advanced communications skills, emotional intelligence, ethical influence, body language and disruptive thinking leading teams towards outstanding results.

A 30-year corporate career as a Senior Manager, in private and public sectors established her reputation for getting things done efficiently through positive and motivated teams. Now an International Speaker, Facilitator, Coach and Author of three books and over 50 training programs; including themes of employee engagement, customer experience, strategic thinking, project leadership, trauma-informed care, mental fitness for success.

Her altruistic and passion projects include giving back to youth self-mastery development, facilitating, and speaking on trauma-informed care empowerment and training "pre-escalation" techniques to 1st responder agencies.

INDEX - ARTICLES / WEB SITES

[i] "Is Your Workplace Tough — or Is It Toxic?" Knowledge@Wharton, August 12, 2015, accessed October 01, 2020.https://knowledge.wharton.upenn.edu/article/is-your-workplace-tough-or-is-it-toxic/

[ii] G. (2017). STATISTICAL REFERENCE GUIDE FOR RECRUITERS 50 HR and Recruiting Statistics for 2017 [Web log post]. Retrieved 2018, from https://resources.glassdoor.com/rs/899-LOT-464/images/50hr-recruiting-and-statistics-2017.pdf

[iii] Adkins, J. (2020, August 25). Employees Want a Lot More From Their Managers. Retrieved October 01, 2020, from https://www.gallup.com/workplace/236570/employees-lot-managers.aspx

[iv] S. (2016). EMPLOYEE JOB SATISFACTION AND ENGAGEMENT Revitalizing a Changing Workforce. Retrieved 2018, from https://www.shrm.org/hr-today/trends-and-forecasting/research-and-surveys/Documents/2016-Employee-Job-Satisfaction-and-Engagement-Report.pdf

[v] Kessler, E. H. (2013). *Encyclopedia of management theory*(ASIN : B00VBV5A9I). Los Angeles: Sage.

[vi] G. (2017). STATISTICAL REFERENCE GUIDE FOR RECRUITERS 50 HR and Recruiting Statistics for 2017 [Web log post]. Retrieved 2018, from https://resources.glassdoor.com/rs/899-LOT-464/images/50hr-recruiting-and-statistics-2017.pdf

[vii] Solow, M., Parker, K., & Chheng, S. (2015, February 28). Culture and engagement The naked organization [Web log post]. Retrieved October 01, 2018, from https://www2.deloitte.com/us/en/insights/focus/human-capital-trends/2015/employee-engagement-culture-human-capital-trends-2015.html

[viii] Kelly, T. (2010). A Positive Approach to Change: The Role of Appreciative Inquiry in Library and Information Organisations. *Australian Academic & Research Libraries, 41*(3), 163-177. doi:10.1080/00048623.2010.10721461
[ix] Institute, P. (2018). What is Project Management? Retrieved October 01, 2018, from https://www.pmi.org/about/learn-about-pmi/what-is-project-management

[x] Newberg, M.D., A., & Waldman, M. (2012, August 01). Why This Word Is So Dangerous to Say or Hear [Web log post]. Retrieved October 01, 2018, from https://www.psychologytoday.com/ca/blog/words-can-change-your-brain/201208/why-word-is-so-dangerous-say-or-hear

[xi] Kelly, T. (2010). A Positive Approach to Change: The Role of Appreciative Inquiry in Library and Information Organisations. *Australian Academic & Research Libraries, 41*(3), 163-177. doi:10.1080/00048623.2010.10721461

[xii] Whitney, D., & Cooperrider, D. (2016). Appreciative Inquiry: A Positive Revolution in Change. *Https://www.academia.edu/4063158/Appreciative_Inquiry_A_Positive_Revolution_in_Change*. doi:10.1002/9781118818480.ch6

[xiii] Cooperrider, D. (2012). What is Appreciative Inquiry? Retrieved October 02, 2018, from http://www.davidcooperrider.com/ai-process/
[xiv] Feffer, M. (2016, April 1). HR's Hard Challenge: When Employees Lack Soft Skills [Web log post]. Retrieved 2018, from https://www.shrm.org/hr-today/news/hr-magazine/0416/pages/hrs-hard-challenge-when-employees-lack-soft-skills.aspx

[xv] Mariotti, A., Robinson, S., & Esen, E. (2017). 2017 Human Capital Benchmarking Report [Web log post]. Retrieved 2018, from https://www.shrm.org/hr-today/trends-and-forecasting/research-and-surveys/Documents/2017-Human-Capital-Benchmarking.pdf

[xvi] Altman, J. (2017, January 19). How Much Does Employee Turnover Really Cost? Retrieved October 02, 2020, from https://www.huffingtonpost.com/entry/how-much-does-employee-turnover-really-cost_us_587fbaf9e4b0474ad4874fb7

[xvii] Toren, Adam. "Hiring for Attitude Over Experience." business.com. business.com, December 2, 2015. https://www.business.com/articles/hiring-for-attitude-over-experience-what-the-numbers-show/.

[xviii] Gaal, Simon Van, Floris P. De Lange, and Michael X Cohen. "The Role of Consciousness in Cognitive Control and Decision Making." *Frontiers in Human Neuroscience* 6 (2012). https://doi.org/10.3389/fnhum.2012.00121.

[xix] Staff, Mayo Clinic. "How to Stop Negative Self-Talk." Mayo Clinic. Mayo Foundation for Medical Education and Research, January 21, 2020. https://www.mayoclinic.org/healthy-lifestyle/stress-management/in-depth/positive-thinking/art-20043950.

[xx] Grohol, John M. "15 Common Cognitive Distortions." Psych Central. Psych Central, June 24, 2019. https://psychcentral.com/lib/15-common-cognitive-distortions/.

[xxi] Merton, Robert. "The Self-Fulfilling Prophecy." Web log. *Www.popularsocialscience.com* (blog). Popular Social Science, December 27, 2012. http://www.popularsocialscience.com/2012/12/27/the-self-fulfilling-prophecy/.

[xxii] MacNeil, James. "Use Verbal Aikido Training To." Verbal Aikido, 2011. http://verbalaikido.com/.

[xxiii] Quote from: D. James Lauber, Verbal Aikido Licensee

[xxiv] Breazeale, Ron. "In-the-Face-Adversity." *Psychology Today* (blog). Sussex Publishers, LLC, March 25, 2011. www.psychologytoday.com/blog/in-the-face-adversity/201103/catastrophic-thinking.

[xxv] Nicholls, A.R., Polman, R.C.J. and Holt, N.L. (2005). The effects of individualized imagery interventions on golf performance and flow states. *Athletic Insight: the Online Journal of Sport Psychology*, 7(1). 16 January 2008, www.athleticinsight.com/Vol7Iss1/ImageryGolfFlow.htm

[xxvi] "Lanny BASSHAM." International Olympic Committee. THE INTERNATIONAL OLYMPIC COMMITTEE, November 26, 2020. http://www.olympic.org/lanny-bassham.

[xxvii] Bender, Todd, Fred Funk, Brady Ellison, and Wendell Cherry. "Fore The Mind – The Mental Program for Golf." Our store for books, audio CDs,, DVD's for mental training. Mental Management Systems. Accessed November 26, 2020. https://www.mentalmanagementstore.com/?ap_id=DeeComms.

[xxviii] Berlin, Heather A. "The Neural Basis of the Dynamic Unconscious." *Neuropsa.org* (blog). The International Neuropsychoanalysis Society, 2011. www.nyu.edu/gsas/dept/philo/faculty/block/papers/BerlinTreatment.pdf.

[xxix] The Boston Consulting Group, In collaboration with. "Towards a Reskilling Revolution." World Economic Forum. The Boston Consulting Group, January 2018. http://www.weforum.org/reports/towards-a-reskilling-revolution.

[xxx] Forum, World Economic. "Skills Stability." The Future of Jobs. World Economic Forum, January 2018. http://reports.weforum.org/future-of-jobs-2016/skills-stability/.

xxxi Ott, Ryan Pendell and Bryant. "3 Daily Actions That Set the World's Best Managers Apart." Gallup.com. Gallup, November 11, 2018. http://news.gallup.com/opinion/gallup/226784/daily-actions-set-world-best-managers-apart.aspx.

xxxii Fox, Tom, and Stephen M.R. Covey. "Stephen M. R. Covey's Guide to Building Trust." *The Washington Post.* July 18, 2013. www.washingtonpost.com/news/on-leadership/wp/2013/07/18/stephen-m-r-coveys-guide-to-building-trust/?utm_term=.115f59d2fe23.

xxxiii Goleman, Daniel. "Empathy 101." Daniel Goleman. Daniel Goleman, OAD. www.danielgoleman.info/empathy-101/.

xxxiv Burton, Neel. "Empathy vs. Sympathy." Psychology Today. Sussex Publishers, May 22, 2015. https://www.psychologytoday.com/us/blog/hide-and-seek/201505/empathy-vs-sympathy.

xxxv White, Martha C. "When Microsoft's CEO Joined the Company 3 Years Ago, He Had an Epiphany That Has Guided His Role Ever Since." Business Insider. Business Insider, October 4, 2017. http://www.businessinsider.com/microsoft-ceo-says-success-has-nothing-to-do-with-your-skills-2017-10.

xxxvi Warren, Kevin. *FINDING L.I.F.E.* Maitland, FL: XULON Press, 2015.

xxxvii "Description of Transactional Analysis and Games by Dr. Eric Berne MD." Eric Berne M.D. The estate of Eric Berne MD, 1999 – 2019, January 28, 2013. http://www.ericberne.com/transactional-analysis/.

xxxviii Berne, Eric. Transactional Analysis in Psychotherapy: a Systematic Individual and Social Psychiatry. Mansfield Centre, CT: Martino Publishing, 2015.

xxxix Harris, Thomas A. *I'm OK, You're OK.* London: Arrow, 2012.

xl Davidson, Richard J., and Sharon Begley. The Emotional Life of Your Brain: How Its Unique Patterns Affect the Way You Think, Feel, and Live--and How You Can Change Them. New York: Plume, 2013.

xli Gupta, Mukesh. Web log. *Http://Innovationexcellence.com/Blog/2016/09/23/Innovation-Starts-with-a-Question/* (blog). Disruptor League, September 23, 2016. https://disruptorleague.wpcomstaging.com/2016/09/23/innovation-starts-with-a-question/.

xlii Inc., Prosci. "The Global Leader in Change Management Solutions." Prosci. Accessed December 9, 2020. http://www.prosci.com/.

xliii Berne, Eric. "Games People Play: Eric Berne: Creator of Transactional Analysis." Eric Berne M.D. The estate of Eric Berne MD, 1999 – 2019, February 15, 2016. http://www.ericberne.com/games-people-play/.

xliv Karpman, Stephen. "A GAME FREE LIFE ." The Official Site of the Karpman Drama Triangle. Stephen Karpman. Accessed March 9, 2018. https://www.karpmandramatriangle.com/.

xlv Zwicky, Arnold. "A Prevalence of Left Handers." Web log. *Arnold Zwicky's Blog* (blog). Arnold Zwicky, December 9, 2015. https://arnoldzwicky.org/2015/12/09/a-prevalence-of-left-handers/.

www.ingramcontent.com/pod-product-compliance
Lightning Source LLC
Chambersburg PA
CBHW052247220526
45471CB00001B/219